Speci

Autism Perspectives:

Musings from the Family of an Autistic Kid

By Brad Eck

With Contributions from:

Abby Printz, Benji Eck, Daniel Eck, Cindy Eck,

Shirley Kohl, and Eddie Eck

Foreword by and Contributions from:

Jeff Johnson, LMFT

Brad Eck

Chadds Ford, PA 19317

www. authorbradeck.com

Ordering Information:

For details, contact info@authorbradeck.com

Print ISBN: 978-1-09835-831-0

eBook ISBN: 978-1-09835-832-7

Printed in the United States of America on SFI Certified paper.

First Edition

Table of Contents

Verses

Lessons

Foreword

By Jeff Johnson, LMFT

Parenting is tough. Parenting a child with special needs can feel impossible, and sometimes is impossible. My experience as a therapist and parent has taught me that no parent should ever be judged; but as parents we all have a responsibility in recognizing our short-comings, flaws, and areas for improvement. We need to work on these for our children, partners, and ourselves. The Eck's story exemplifies this struggle and journey towards change and growth and highlights the impossible moments, the strange and unpredictable moments, and the moments to treasure despite the challenges.

I applaud Brad and his family for talking about their struggles and lessons learned and hope that others find hope in their story and recognize that we can all make changes that improve how we intervene with our family members and how we move through the challenges, difficulties, and impossibilities to be better people and family members for each other.

I am glad to see that the Ecks have moved towards a better way of interacting and connecting with one another and hope that others can learn or glean something that will help them in their own journey with their child or family member.

Introduction

Proverbs 22:6 (MSG):

"Point your kids in the right direction - when they're old they won't be lost."

When my son Daniel was five years old, he was diagnosed with high-functioning autism. From the beginning we committed to mainstreaming Daniel by giving him access to all the typical things in life instead of yielding to his special needs. This was not for the faint of heart (or wallet). It was a very trying and expensive process. But little did we know then, the diagnosis would open doors and address much of the help needed and many of those associated costs.

As time marched on, we realized that among all the little daily things we faced with Daniel, each year we usually had one major story to call out as unique and, well, outrageous. That is when the idea of this book began: a collection of memories. But as time moved on and our passion toward mentoring and investing in others grew, it became apparent that we needed to share our lessons, failures, and most importantly, our successes.

There were a lot of things we could have done differently, but we raised him in the best way we could with the resources that were available. In the end, it will be Daniel who chooses to grow and behave in the way he sees best. He often chooses to learn lessons the hard way, but perhaps those hard life experiences are what will best shape and ground him.

Today Daniel lives on his own as a functioning adult. He lives in a house with roommates and is trying to find his way in this big world of decisions. He still flows through a large range of emotions quite quickly. This is exacerbated by his refusal to leverage support in therapy and medicine. He also refuses to let others know that he is autistic, thereby forcing himself to work at normalcy. That has benefits, but also comes with its own issues. But he feels that is the right thing for him. He continues to learn to manage his autistic tendencies and works to take care of himself.

And us? Well, we remain teachable and humble to our God in heaven. He gave us Daniel, knowing this would be difficult, but has always walked alongside us every second of every day. Faith was the only thing that got us through some days.

We know we must let Daniel fly, and we have encouraged him to take flight and become a man. We are proud of him and the man he is becoming.

God is sovereign

Yes, we were the right parents for Daniel. But he was also the right child for us.

What to Expect while Reading this Book

You will find that the reading style of this book is a little different than typical. To give you some insight into this, consider the following guidelines while reading.

Each chapter starts with a scripture verse to build context for the stories and from which each lesson will be based. We often forget to search out truth from the Bible. But recognizing that all things come from heaven above is a good first step in living a worthwhile life.

Most times the stories start with the actual event occurrence and then it is followed by context and background.

This book is primarily drawn from stories from my own (Dad's) perspective. However, as every member of a family sees things differently, I wanted to present you with different perspectives on the stories represented. So where appropriate, I have often included others' memories to help tell the story or give additional perspective (contributor details can be found at the end of the book). These are called out in the text by the person's relationship to Daniel (e.g., "...from Daniel's sister...").

Amid the stories are single statements of emotion (e.g., "Relieved.") These are not meant to tell the reader how he should feel, but for the reader to understand the emotions that the author felt at the time of the event.

At the end of each story is a lesson that can be drawn from the experience. Perhaps the lesson resonates with you, or maybe you can pull something different from the story. Either way, it is vital that we take the opportunity to pull from our experiences so that we may not only live our own lives better but may also help to improve others' lives as well.

Finally, while the first chapter focuses on some family background to provide appropriate context to the stories which follow, the remaining chapters correspond to the respective year of Daniel's life.

Pre-birth / Family

Job 36:26 (MSG):

"Take a long, hard look. See how great he is - infinite, greater than anything you could ever imagine or figure out! "He pulls water up out of the sea, distills it, and fills up his rain-cloud cisterns. Then the skies open up and pour out soaking showers on everyone. Does anyone have the slightest idea how this happens? How he arranges the clouds, how he speaks in thunder? Just look at that lightning, his sky-filling light show illumining the dark depths of the sea! These are the symbols of his sovereignty, his generosity, his loving care. He hurls arrows of light, taking sure and accurate aim. The High God roars in the thunder, angry against evil."

After my wife and I were married in 1992 in West Linn, Oregon, we experienced a great first couple of years enjoying each other and integrating into the idea of marriage and what that looked like for us. We were living in Seattle; I was working for a software company and my wife in retail clothing. We had a great church home and a good surrounding of friends. Then after three years, because of the rain as well as other personal reasons, we decided to move to Texas. It was then we struggled: struggled to find friends; struggled to find a good church home; and struggled to really settle well.

Then, in July of 1994, she and I found out we were expecting a baby and while it was not planned, we were nonetheless excited.

A bit later that month we found ourselves on a plane visiting family in California. About midway through the flight, my wife went to the restroom. On her return, she stated something was wrong. Being a first-time mother, she did not know how to convey what she felt intuitively was a problem with the baby.

We called the flight attendant and, appropriately alarmed, she promptly went into action – basically getting her crew prepped to have an ambulance available on arrival.

Pissed.

The flight attendants announced the emergency. They asked for people to allow us to exit the flight before anyone got out of their seats.

"Bing!" The bell went off. Instead of waiting for us as they had been asked, the usual scramble to exit ensued, leaving us caught up in the traffic. When we finally got off the plane, the stretcher was waiting for us and my wife was wheeled up through the jetway.

I cannot imagine my sister-in-law's horror when she saw the stretcher come out of the jetway and realized I was running alongside. Oh, what a sight! Later, at the hospital, the explanations ensued, but the utter dismay of not knowing must have been alarming. After all, they did not even know she was pregnant.

Sorrow.

We lost our baby that day. My wife remained healthy, but our baby was gone. As life begins at inception, we believe we will see our child again one day in heaven and we so look forward to the day we will meet him or her up there. Nevertheless, it was a sad day and a horrible way to start a vacation with family. Still, our sovereign God knew that the best place for us was with my brother and sister-in-law.

...from Daniel's sister...

Like most people, I do not remember much of the first few years of my life. My parents have told me stories and my dad has related to me various facts, including that I was a C-section birth, I was born not long after my mother had a miscarriage, and that for all intents and purposes, I was a relatively "easy" baby.

I remember for a while wondering what it would have been like should my mother not have miscarried that day on the plane. It bothered me for quite a few years of my childhood and sometimes even during my later years. I wondered if it would have been a boy or a girl. I remember telling my parents that I would have liked having an older brother. I never really considered the fear, trauma, and sadness those words might have brought rushing back to both my parents.

I never truly understood what happened to my mother until I read it in my father's first chapter. He had never fully explained to me what happened, and now when I read those words, I cannot help the tears that stream down my cheeks. I can just imagine the fear in my dad's eyes, the dread in my mom's voice, the terror and confusion in my aunt when she saw them.

The doctor said, "No sex for two months." And then, as odd as it may be, only eight months later we were in a hospital in Fort Worth for the birth of our first, our daughter – at full term. I never could add it up and make it work, but then again, I have never been one to question the amazing power of our Lord. To me, nothing is impossible for Him, and our daughter is nothing less than a miracle child for us.

Agony.

We went into the hospital on Monday early and prepared. At 9, they took my wife away for prep and said they would call me in for the birth in about fifteen minutes. And time went on. And on. And on. At 10, they finally called me in apologizing for the delay, but said they were having "some issues." At 10:15, my wife had a seizure and they said in a flurry, "He needs to leave, and we need to take the baby out now. Knock her out," as they yanked me out of the room. I can still feel the utter confusion and pain of the moment. My hand was over my mouth and I was in shock of the unknown. I stood outside the nursery just waiting. Minutes felt like hours.

And then she came. My beautiful daughter brought so much relief. But what of my darling wife?

A few minutes later the doctor came out and said she was fine but resting. A while later they brought my wife back into the hospital room, groggy, but awake. She spent the expected few days recovering in the hospital and taking care of our newborn. In the end, all were healthy, and everything was fine.

...from Daniel's sister (continued)...

My mother is one of the strongest women I know. Though we always struggled to share the emotional bond that most other girls have with their mothers, I always respected her and was sometimes awed by her. She never backed down, never let fear or anxiety win the best of her. She birthed me eight months later, and though it was God's will that put me inside her so soon after the miscarriage, I think it was her desire and sheer willpower that pushed me out into the world.

Joy.

We did not find out what really happened that day. There was conjecture everywhere but no conclusions. We were just happy to be healthy – and that was enough. We took our daughter home and began the plight of being new parents. We had a basic support system built up by this time, but we lived quite far from our church home, so it was difficult and distant. Most importantly, my wife and I made a choice to raise our kids ourselves. This left the burden of financial support for the family solely on my shoulders, and the burden of the day-to-day work of raising the children to my wife.

...from Daniel's sister (continued)...

Her only "easy" birth was my brother, Daniel, and the rest of his life was far from easy. Yet, through all the pain and heartache, through all the difficulties she has faced, she never gave up on myself or my brothers, she never gave up on her husband, and most importantly, she never gave up on God. Her stubbornness, and mine as well, has been the cause of so much strife between the two of us. Yet at the end of the day, I thank God for that stubbornness, and I thank Him even more that He blessed me with it. If my mother were not that way, I do not think she would have continued to have three children, or to do her best to give my brother the life that he deserved, or to stick it out with my father and show the true meaning of marriage and the promise they both made to God. Without my mother's strength, I would not have become the woman I am today.

The first year of our daughter's life was difficult for us as a couple. I took on a second job and my wife adapted into the role of a stay-at-home mom. The transition of parenthood converged with the reality of typical early marriage disagreements to create serious tension in our relationship. My wife and I were not just opposites; we were completely opposite, and it showed.

Every.

Single.

Day.

Alongside my personal anger issues, all of this made for a rough start. And to add to it, it was during this time that we decided to move back to the Northwest.

Marriage incompatibilities

Incompatibilities in marriage are a given. That is why pre-marital counseling exists. My wife and I, due to the extent of those incompatibilities, endured an unusually high level of conflict in the early years of our marriage, and still often struggle today.

My wife and I are trained marriage mentors and have advised many couples on strategies for a successful marriage. Part of that process is an assessment (e.g., FOCCUS, SIMBUS, etc.) – an independent measurement of compatibilities deemed vital to the success of a marriage. As we would find out in much more detail later, we were incompatible in so many ways – in more ways than would be considered healthy. So much so that if we were being mentored today, we would expect the mentor to do everything in his power to dissuade the marriage.

However, the one thing that mattered most is likely the only reason we are still together today – we are **committed**, beyond everything else, to make it work. And we know that will only happen when we each lean on God as our ultimate source of strength, rather than each other.

A final note here: after our relationship with God, **our** marriage comes **first** and the relationship with our children comes second. It is incredibly important that our kids need to understand that my wife is number one, as I am to her. They do not have to like it, but they do need to understand it.

When we are aligned, we together can most effectively show our children how to live in this world.

When I look for investment advice, I seek out people who are successful in their financial lives. When I look for spiritual advice, I seek out those who are revered in theological strength and the application thereof. And when I seek out marital help, I look to those who are successful in their marriage; in the raising of their family; and the love in which they show to each other.

If you are married, your spouse is number one. If you are married again, your spouse in number one. And if you are married a third time (etc.), your spouse is number one. Let your children (and stepchildren, etc.) know and be clear: do not ever let them come between you.

Edwin Cole's book "Communication, Sex, and Money"[1] is a classic best-seller addressing three of the biggest problems faced in marriage. While those are true, your relationship priorities and your commitment to those priorities will be the greatest influence carrying you through those trials.

Good or bad.

You choose.

---

[1] Edwin Cole, *Communication, Sex, and Money*, 2nd edition (Word and Spirit Resources, LLC, June 1, 2002)

Birth Year and Age 1: The Beginning

> **Ecclesiastes 4:9-12 (MSG):**
>
> *"It's better to have a partner than go it alone. Share the work, share the wealth. And if one falls down, the other helps, But if there's no one to help, tough! Two in a bed warm each other. Alone, you shiver all night. By yourself you're unprotected. With a friend you can face the worst. Can you round up a third? A three-stranded rope isn't easily snapped."*

Relief.

That is the best way to express the wonderful birth of our first son, our second-born child. Daniel was born in November of 1997 in Bellevue, WA, and we were thankful to have no drama. No issues. Just a normal birth. We had advised the medical team of the concerns from our daughter's birth and they had some ideas so took appropriate defensive actions and, for all we knew, addressed them.

My wife was amazing, and our beautiful boy was born a healthy 8 pounds 9 ounces. Overjoyed, for my wife had succeeded with her first VBAC (vaginal birth after Cesarean) with no difficulties. This is an important consideration since smooth is not how we would characterize Daniel's life since his birth.

Thankful.

God is sovereign and above ALL men

Trust in Him. Trust in His sovereignty. Know that He is in control no matter what you say or do. Lean into Him. There is amazing freedom in accepting that someone else is in control of your life and He has greater authority in this world than you ever will. It alleviates anxiety and gives you a peace in every situation that is simply beyond explanation and understanding.

Flustered.

Please. Shut. Up!

Blood curdling screaming.

Constant crying.

"Will we ever sleep?"

Daniel cried a lot in those days due to what we believed was gas. He was clearly uncomfortable - always. As parents, we had to learn to adapt. It turned out this was a sort of preparation for what was to come. We had to research. We had to find a solution.

In the end, only time served as the resolution as it eventually worked itself out. I suspect the many attempts at diet and lifestyle change ultimately influenced it, but we never really put our finger on the solution. We just know he had a hard start in life.

"Why couldn't he be as good as our daughter?"

"Why is this so difficult?"

"What are we doing wrong?"

The cycle of questions is endless when things are difficult in our lives, right? Thankfully, we were back at our church home and had a great support system through the initial difficulties we faced with Daniel. Most importantly, my wife had a great support system of other women helping her work through all the transitions.

Get help

- *Build up a support network. We are social individuals, and we need engagement from others. Trials will come – prepare for them. And part of that preparation should be to have a group of individuals / couples who are close enough to you that they will step in and help when the time is needed. And, in return, you can be that for them as well.*

- *Additionally, get your kids on a schedule and stick to it. As babies, we had them on schedules in the first weeks. This can be difficult ... until they adapt to the schedule. Go through the pain – it is so worth it. They will cry and want you to come. Honor the schedule. There are plenty of resources out there to define it (per age), but I cannot encourage you enough to make this happen. It will dramatically shift your experience with a young child.*

- *Finally, set boundaries and apply them consistently. What that means to everyone is different, but the simple fact is that kids need (and want) boundaries (but will never tell you so). But boundaries mean nothing if there are no consequences when those boundaries are crossed – so uphold them. How you do that is up to you, but consequences are vital for your children to associate action with consequence.*

Age 2: Steady On

Discontent.

We originally left Seattle in '93 because of the rain. Returning in '96 was risky, but we decided it was worth it. And really, my wife wanted to be near home. But in 1999 we had over 100+ days straight of rain. With a five-year-old and two-year-old running around in the house, my wife was going nuts. In fact, Daniel had hit his "terrible twos" (which, by the way, he never really exited). By this time, my wife and I had started working to resolve our "oppositeness" and our marriage was settling down so that we were in a better place together, which was good given the trying times that were ahead.

But then we had to make a difficult decision.

"Let's find where we want to spend the rest of our lives together."

We wanted to settle down and raise our kids and we knew it could not be in the Northwest. We also knew SoCal was not an option (where I grew up) for various reasons (including a ridiculous cost of living). And Fort Worth or Arlington, Texas were both simply brown, ugly, and the bugs were just too much for us.

So, I found a job as a consultant; we bought a truck and travel trailer; put the house up for sale; and headed out. We mapped out a "V" across the US – starting in the Northwest and ending in the Northeast with the vertex in Dallas. On Monday morning, I would fly to wherever I needed to be and fly home on Friday. I trusted my wife completely to assess the area for our long-term desires and needs. So, we would pack up and

leave on Saturday morning for a 5-to-10-hour drive to the next destination. During the week, my wife would throw the kids in the car and drive around checking out the area to assess the viability of our long-term home. We did this for three months when we landed at a friend's property on the east side of Dallas, Texas (going from west to east in the South, Dallas is where the brown half of the country turns green).

...from Daniel's sister...

I do not remember much else from Seattle. My parents did a lot of searching for a new place, and before I knew it, my dad and I were riding in a box truck on our way to Rockwall, Texas. If there is anywhere in Texas that I would love to go back to and stay, it would be that city. I fell in love with all of it; the land, the people, the nature. Texas has its own culture, and it was mine.

My parents found this great house in a great area, and I was happy. I loved my school, loved my neighbors, and loved my church. I remember pool parties, biking down this big hill in the neighborhood, playing "cops and robbers" with my neighbor across the street, and landscaping and installing our own playground in the backyard. I remember forging friendships at church that would last us for years to come as we continued our habit of moving every few years. But most of all, I remember noticing for the first time that Daniel did not seem like other kids his age.

Flexibility and adaptability

They say the only reliable thing in life is change. Taking that one step further, we as humans tend to do everything we can to minimize change and the impact of it in our lives. We live defensively in that way.

But status quo is stagnant. I get it - when things are good in life, our comfort zone kicks in and we do not want change, and for sure we do not seek it out. But what if we just embraced it? Or better yet, what if you woke up in the morning and prayed, "God, what new do You have in store for me today?" How would you handle change coming at you daily?

"Well, surprise, surprise, surprise!" The reality of pregnancy comes fully frontal when you cannot get through the door of the trailer bathroom! Those things are small! So, our pursuit of a new place to live came to a screeching halt. We began looking for a house where we were and honestly, found a great place. In time, we fell in love with Rockwall, Texas and truly planned to make it our long-term home.

Fear. (Again.)

In 2000, we went into the hospital to have our third. Prep went well, and then it happened – my wife had another seizure.

A planned vaginal birth, her labor extended, and she began getting tired.

But! Thanks to the hard work and brilliance of our anesthesiologist, a solution was found. After about an hour of research, he came back and said he believed my wife was having a rare allergic reaction to one of the preparatory drugs. He gave her a counteracting drug and immediately the affects subsided. We found out this was a regional drug and that explained why we had not faced this problem in WA. It was likely also the cause of the problem with our daughter's birth.

...from Daniel's sister (continued)...

While there in Rockwall, my mother gave birth to my younger brother.

I remember my dad explaining to Daniel and me in the hospital that all three of us were named after influential people in the Bible. I also remember him being worried at the beginning, but eventually relieved.

I later learned that my younger brother's birth had been dangerously complicated. I thank God every day that my mom was able to get through all three births and move on to parent us.

Exhausted.

But now my wife was tired. Really exhausted. And she had to give birth normally. After some coaxing, our youngest came into this world a healthy baby. Both he and mom came through it fine. And we were most thankful for answers to why things had been so difficult for our first and third births.

Snip.

Three children were enough.

Always be thankful

Compared to the world around us, we have so many blessings. I often say, "first world problem" when responding to someone who is complaining about their "struggles." Do not get me wrong, I understand difficulties, trials, etc., but in the context of having a home and food and other necessities, our trials often pale in comparison to others' struggles for basic human needs.

Be thankful. Gratefulness is an excellent character trait. It crafts contentment; it encourages humility, and even fosters kindness and charity.

You are blessed.

Age 3: Cunning

I was in our entranceway heading to the kitchen. Seeing movement out of the top of my eye, I looked up and my heart came to a screeching halt!

Holy. Crap!

"HONEEEEEEEEEEY!!!! I need you to come here NOW!"

Looking up I saw Daniel teetering on the loft banister *far* above my head. Oh! The thoughts that ran through my head!

"How did he get up there?"

"Jesus, help me!"

"What craziness ensues?"

But then fight mode kicked in and I knew I had to react. My wife came running in as I stood looking up not daring to take my eyes off him. "Babe, please go grab your son while I stand here and make sure he doesn't fall!" I realized my presence could not stop the fall, of course, but it at least might allay the landing. My wife scrambled up the stairs and managed to sweep him away to safety.

Our house in Texas had high ceilings and so by the time you accounted for the second-floor depth and half wall, we were looking at about fifteen feet – or should I say, Daniel was looking about fifteen foot down to a ceramic tile floor.

It was then we realized a human's natural fear of heights was of little concern to him. Daniel had, at the age of three, managed to conclude that if he grabbed bean bag chairs and stacked them, he could do things requiring extra height. In this case, get on top of a four-foot wall and crawl to the end, despite it being only four inches wide (and fifteen feet to the floor).

...from Daniel's sister...

It took a little bit of time, but not nearly as long as you might think. Daniel started showing signs of strangeness early on in life, but for a while it just seemed that he had this weird knack for doing crazy and elaborate things. A lot of people argue that autism mutes intelligence in a person, but those of us who have worked closely with autistic people will tell you it is quite the opposite. Autistic people can be quite brilliant, and in this case, Daniel is no exception.

Still at home in Texas, Daniel began to show his creativity when it came to getting things he wanted. And that fear of heights and danger that plagues most people was nonexistent in Daniel. I have lost count of how many times we would find him hanging from something high enough to cause serious injury should he fall. At three years old, he stacked chairs and climbed onto a four-inch-wide banister and crawled to the end looking over a fifteen-foot drop to the main floor. Freaking crazy.

Do not fear fear

Fear can be a crutch in this life. But it also has some positive uses. In this case, the natural fear of heights is there for protection. Well, at least, for those in whom it exists. For Daniel, it did not. And for a dad that struggles so desperately with heights himself, this could be a big challenge.

Raising Daniel and knowing that he was not afraid to climb anything made for some interesting moments. This one, on the banister, was only the beginning.

But fear can also be a problem. I have personally dealt with my fear of heights by facing it head on. Deterring it from accomplishing personal goals (and bucket lists) is very beneficial. I encourage you to assess those things that "bubble up" anxiety in you when you think of them. And then, attack them. Do not let fear win. One step at a time, move toward addressing that fear. And it helps tremendously to have someone alongside you supporting and encouraging you along the way.

Perhaps that fear is stopping a bad habit. I just have two words for you: be better. You are a decision away from the next step that will help you overcome.

On Edge.

It was also at this age where Daniel's intelligence began to show in other ways. Having learned to ride a bike at age two (with training wheels), one day he came running into the house and said he had removed his training wheels and was riding his bike normally without them.

Age three.

With no help from us.

Oh, God, please help us.

While this was seemingly amazing news and joyous in so many ways, it also created a sense of fear in us parents. We then began to anticipate the myriads of ways our kid could misuse this intelligence.

That level of intelligence without the balance of concern for safety is a major accident just waiting to happen. Well, in our case, it also led to many dollars of repair work over the forthcoming years. This is when the cat and mouse game began between him and me. From here on out, he was hell-bent on breaking the rules, and I was left reacting to and anticipating his next actions.

I have long struggled with an inability to manage frustration and instead allowing it to trigger into anger. This has played out in many ways, but the brunt is borne in an emotional impact by those closest to me. Daniel's ability to find those triggers was uncanny, and my inability to manage them took a heavy toll on me and the family as a whole.

...from Daniel's sister (continued)...

Daniel also started to understand the basic mechanics of things. He took the training wheels off his bike by himself and started picking and pulling things apart, with or without tools. Unfortunately, not all those things were his toys. As he grew older, his natural ability to take things apart or break them down became a huge issue and a constant battle between him and my father. The "cat-and-mouse game", as my father called it, consisted of my father locking something, and Daniel getting into it anyways. Things continued to escalate, locks and security measures started to get expensive, and all the while, Daniel proved his ability to get into anything he wanted. I am glad he has not decided to become a professional thief, because if he figured out how to escape without getting caught, he would be scary good at it.

Anger management

I was a horrible example of anger management. From watching other people throughout my life, I had learned that getting angry and lashing out was a perfectly acceptable form of managing trials in life. It is not.

Unfortunately, my family bore the brunt of this. They saw me get angry at the smallest of things with no ability to manage it. I recognized it early and consistently reached out for help (professionally and personally). But nothing worked. I was unable to find a way to properly manage this.

Simply put, the struggle continued because there was no personal motivation to address and fix it. There was no (unmanageable) cost to my anger ... at least, none that I could find.

In time (and with much therapy), I would realize the damage I had been doing to my kids and wife through my example of anger and violence. My kids' inability to manage their own anger ended up being a slap in my own face. One that took me until Daniel was seventeen before I could truly overcome. It still gets the best of me at times, but I continue to process and grow through this, knowing that I am a better example for every time I manage my anger appropriately.

If you are struggling with anger, or any other bad habit, do not attack it alone. Get help. Professionally AND personally. You need the guidance of an expert as well as the support of a friend.

Concern.

It was at age three that we also began seeing something else. While Daniel's gross motor skills were amazing, his fine motor skills were not so good. Additionally, his speech was very delayed. We had taught him (as we did all our kids) basic sign language for things he needed before he could speak, but even at age two he was barely saying words. It was not until age four that he could put words together to form thoughts, but his speech was still continuously delayed.

We tried to work with the school to understand what was happening but all they did was a basic speech test and somehow, in the ridiculousness of it all, they said he was normal.

...from Daniel's sister (continued)...

The family started to realize that Daniel was no ordinary child. While he showed this amazing ability with tools and his understanding of the functionality of objects, as well as an increasing interest in technology, his speech was not keeping up. He was barely saying anything, whereas other children his age were forming full sentences. He would sometimes communicate with us through sign language, but even that was difficult as he often could not figure out the right sign, even though he had done it before. His fine motor skills seemed to be getting more worse by comparison, and my parents grew concerned. At the time, the school's testing somehow showed he was quite normal. We all know the truth now, but it makes me concerned to wonder how many other children were misdiagnosed and for how long did they have to live with it?

The struggles with Daniel that began in that year would put a strain on our marriage in ways we could never have anticipated. The frustrations with Daniel sent me spiraling in frustration and then anger, and my wife struggled to manage both Daniel and I amid everything going on. This caused a cycle of introspection – one which typically led to more self-reliance. And while in-and-of-itself that can be a great character trait, in the context of marriage and family, self-reliance counters the engagement needed to succeed as a family unit.

The dangers of isolation

We are relational beings. And while a small level of introspection is healthy, isolation brings danger.

Besides the clear impact to your physical health (including decreasing life span) isolation can lead to loneliness, depression, and a general dissatisfaction with the social aspects of one's life.

The basis for quality of life is engaging with others. Balance your life and engage. Isolation is self-destructive.

Age 4: Blue Toilet Paper Running

2 Samuel 6:3-7 (MSG):

"They placed the Chest of God on a brand-new oxcart and removed it from Abinadab's house on the hill. Uzzah and Ahio, Abinadab's sons, were driving the new cart loaded with the Chest of God, Ahio in the lead and Uzzah alongside the Chest. David and the whole company of Israel were in the parade, singing at the top of their lungs and playing mandolins, harps, tambourines, castanets, and cymbals. When they came to the threshing floor of Nacon, the oxen stumbled, so Uzzah reached out and grabbed the Chest of God. God blazed in anger against Uzzah and struck him hard because he had profaned the Chest. Uzzah died on the spot, right alongside the Chest."

Unease.

"Where's Daniel?"

That statement sparks fear into the heart of every parent. That moment when you realize there is an unsettling silence and you have absolutely no idea where your child is. By this time, Daniel had successfully figured out how to break through standard door locks, and any attempt to keep him out of anywhere was a constant game of cat and mouse.

We had put keyhole / latch locks at the top of any door in the house of which we needed Daniel to stay out. This worked brilliantly for a while, until he concluded the bean bag chair trick would work again. One. Two. Three. Four. I have no idea how he did it, but he stacked four bean bag chairs up and climbed to the top of a standard door (he is only four!).

Then he proceeded to unlatch the door, climb down, open the door, and get in the room.

What did he find? Well, we were painting his room. Midnight blue. So, there was one gallon of paint on the floor (closed, of course, not that it mattered), with a four-inch paint brush and a paint can key. I suspect this was easy for him, but it still amazes me that he grabbed that key and got the can open. And then our little artist proceeded to paint everything EXCEPT the wall (obviously). The trim, the carpet, whatever. Thankfully, we had removed the furniture (in prep to work on the floor) and we were getting rid of the carpet. But nevertheless, we had quite the clean-up job to do.

Note to self: do not paint dark colors if you have this risk because recovery is brutal.

Safety practices / adaption

In addition to latching the doors high so that he could not get in, we had to deal with an even more pressing safety issue – Daniel would get out of his room at night. And to make things worse, he would even leave the house.

*So, in an effort to keep him safest, and with few options at hand, we opted to trade one risk for another – we locked him **in** his room. This ended up being a very long-term strategy, and ultimately supported by the psychologists and doctors as the safest option, as odd and uncomfortable that it was at the time. Little did we know how beneficial this would be in time.*

Sometimes we exhaust all our own resources in trying to find solutions. This is a tangible use of having a support network. Make some calls, talk through the issue, come up with ideas. Engage with others and get their perspectives. You might just come up with some amazing options for dealing with issues. While the input you receive might be completely counter to your own ideas, you will have greater confidence with others' affirmations of what may seem like far-fetched suggestions.

Later that same year my wife and I opted to go on our first cruise together. We were celebrating our 10-year anniversary (a little early mind you) and were excited to get away for a rare opportunity without our kids. We invited the children's grandma and auntie to our house to kid-watch and then enthusiastically left for our vacation.

...from Daniel's Gramma...

Shortly after September 11, 2001 in NY, Brad and his wife went on a cruise and asked Brad's sister to come to their house in Texas and watch the children. Since Grampa and I were staying at an RV Park near their house, Brad's sister asked if I would come and help her.

We went to the kitchen to make pizza and asked Daniel if he wanted to help. I put him on a chair next to me and we began to make dinner together. He then let me know that he needed to go potty. So, I helped him down and he ran to the bathroom. A short time later, after feeling uneasy about the extended time Daniel had been gone, I asked Brad's sister to go check on him. As he was going to check on him, she stepped into the hallway and realized water had submerged the carpet. She yelled for me and I came running. I went in and the toilet was overflowing. I turned off the water behind the toilet and we found an entire roll of toilet paper in the toilet causing an overflow once it was flushed.

With the water turned off, we quickly realized the water had flowed down the hallway and into the master bedroom, the majority into the living room, the laundry room, and even the office.

We contacted a company to clean up the mess. Upon completion, they placed fans and heaters throughout the soaked areas to help dry the carpet.

Now mind you, any young kid has a curiosity that can sometimes be, well, destructive. Daniel's weapon this time? A (full) roll of toilet paper strategically placed in a way that completely plugged the toilet drain. And while one might look at this as typical boy behavior, a parent must also weigh the deception and the cover up involved. And while everyone was a bit shaken, I suspect this was the point at which our extended family began to really see and understand the depths of Daniel's purposeful deceptions.

...from Daniel's Gramma...

The next morning, Daniel and I were sitting on the top step of the stairway talking. He heard the noise of the fans and heaters and made the statement that he had caused the damage. I explained to him that the toilet could not handle all the toilet paper and it caused the toilet to plug up, which then caused the water to overflow. I told him that in the future he should ask for help as soon as he sees a problem. I could tell by his response that he felt bad, understood, and was sorry.

I just hope auntie had him wash his hands before he helped with dinner!

Wash your hands!

There are many little lessons that can come from this story, but as I write we are all globally reeling with a surge in COVID cases.

So, wash your hands. And geez, teach your kids to as well. It is stunning to see how many people go into public bathrooms and do not do this simple thing.

Ugh.

Pandemic or not, teaching your children basic hygiene is critical to their health and safety.

During that same time period, Daniel's grandpa was also visiting and experienced a situation addressing the need for honesty.

...from Daniel's Grampa...

Daniel was apparently up and about early one morning and needed to go to the bathroom. By the time we were up, we opened his bedroom door and as I walked into the room, I knew something was amiss. Know what I mean? He was suspiciously still and very quiet - unlike his usual self which would get out of bed and into the world of wonder and exploration.

I confronted Daniel about what I sensed was going on. He did not want to respond so I let him know all was well and he could trust me with anything he wanted to tell me. So, surprising me, he laid it all out. He had pooped into a shoe and then proceeded to roll the stuff into small balls like the candy treat "Whoppers". Then he hid them all around the room – in socks – between the mattresses – in other shoes – in the springs under the mattress – etc.

Not sure to this day if we got them all. Egad! Nevertheless, he "told" me ALL. I wanted to laugh but the scene was too unpleasant.

"Boys will be boys" is a common colloquialism that might come to mind here. Some might normalize this event, but in the context of the larger picture of us still trying to determine what was going on in Daniel's mind, this was yet another puzzle piece. And as we would later find out, was instrumental in our ultimate determination that he could not connect action with consequence.

...from Daniel's Grampa (continued)...

To this day I am still so very surprised he was willing to tell me the whole truth and then even help me in the "search and rescue." I did go one more step and ensured him later of the necessity for him to always tell the truth as he knew it and not to be afraid of the consequences. As I used to, and so often, have to tell his father, aunt, and uncle, "be sure of this - daddy WILL find out the truth."

Connecting action with consequence

Something so simple – connecting action with consequence. We all understand this almost intuitively – either because we learned it from our parents, or we figured out that is the way the world works.

But Daniel did not get it. Repetition helped, but only so much. He really could not connect the dots, and this made for very difficult learning through his life. And, unfortunately, peaked my frustration levels more often than not.

Teach your kids this very simple concept. Their actions have consequence – good or bad. Drive it home. Learning this one on their own can be brutal and costly.

Confidence.

Early on I had a specific whistle (just a sharp burst of air through my circled lips in a specific tone) that my kids knew was a call to return to me. I used this sparingly, and mostly only for security concerns. But when they heard it, they knew to come (this took much repetition with swift and effective discipline.) Unfortunately for his grandpa, he could not replicate the whistle.

"Grampa, can we go for a walk?", Daniel said. "Sure, let's go." He and Daniel left and started walking around the block. Grampa said that after the first turn, Daniel ran ahead a little bit. He called Daniel back, and all was well. A little later Daniel ran ahead a little farther. Grampa called him back and he came. The third time, though, Daniel ran around the corner beyond his sight and did not come back. Grampa, in pain from recent arthroscopic surgery on his right knee, tried to run after him but simply could not keep up and quickly realized his helplessness. Scared of what might occur and where Daniel might go, he rounded the last corner praying Daniel would be at the house.

As if nothing was wrong, there he was sitting on the porch waiting for Grampa.

Trying to relay to our sitters how to handle Daniel has always been difficult. We can tell them of his deceit, we can convey the stories of disobedience, and we can express the extent of his defiance. But every time it will be something different. In the end, we simply had to say, "Be defensive and don't trust him."

Obedience

Obedience is so important. Important for many reasons, but one not so obvious area is that it can be a deterrent to danger.

It was then I began to understand a troubling story from the Bible. The one in which a man was killed for his good intentions. One day the Israeli people were traveling from one place to the next. God had clear directions on the handling of his Ark of the Covenant – directions which had clear consequences. That fateful day, one of the oxen carrying the ark stumbled. A man walking next to it reached out to catch the Ark intending to stop it from falling to the ground. God struck him dead. Immediately.

It is a brutal story which I struggled with for so long, but when my kids were young it became increasingly clear to me what it meant. **God is not interested in my intentions, but my actions.** *While he cares about my heart, it is what I do that matters. And what this man did was disobey. His heart was in the right place, but he did not obey. I liken this to a kid who inadvertently kicks his friend's ball across a busy street. His intention to run out and get his friends ball to make sure it is not lost is pure and right, but the consequence of doing it can be fatal.*

In time, the whistle became a way to get their attention, and the discipline was no longer necessary. In fact, today it is used more as a way to find each other in crowds, etc. But in the beginning, I needed something, anything, that would get their attention immediately and have them stop and find me. It was for their safety. And it worked. And many times, we avoided risky problems because they had learned to obey.

Age 5: Artistic Deception

Shock.

"Mommy, come look at what I did!" as he stared up with dark brown paint on his hands, face, etc.

"WHAT!"

Swooping him up into her arms to avoid paint getting anywhere else (except herself of course), my wife followed his directions into the upstairs bathroom only to find paint, once again, everywhere: bathtub, toilet, walls, sinks, etc.

Daniel had found mama's stash of art supplies and grabbed the container of hobby paint. Thankfully, it was water based and most of what he painted was washable. But wow, what that kid can do with a pint of paint is stunning.

...from Daniel's sister...

Daniel had a strange obsession with crafts during his younger years, and more than once decided to get into stashes of paint to get it everywhere. Now, granted, that is very similar to many young children, so by themselves, these incidents do not seem as alarming. But each time Daniel was punished, and each time he would do almost the exact same thing again. This was another pattern that caused my parents to worry over him.

Let your kids thrive

One might conclude that we had an artist on our hand. Far from it. What we had was a kid who got into anything he could get his hands on. Today it was paint, tomorrow something else.

We have always encouraged our kids to chase after their natural talents. In time, Daniel would find his. Do not lose sight of this when incidents such as this take you down a path that will not be pursued. Listen and watch. **They** *have a path – and it is not likely your path. Your job is to guide and empower them to blossom in their own way.*

Too many dads are guilty of pushing their children in a certain direction – be it sports, or medicine, or whatever. And moms can be just as guilty in guiding their kids in their own desired direction.

Be sensitive to what they love, AND why they love it. Ignoring either of these will likely send you down the wrong path.

I encourage people, when searching out their personal mission in life, to find the convergence of talent, skill, and passion. It is there where you will be most happy and successful. The same holds true for your kids, but the skills need to be learned. You can help by introducing them to a breadth of choices, rather than zooming in on one or two, and helping them find the right ones for them.

Disbelief.

"Eck residence?" I answered the phone in my customary fashion. "Yes, this is the pro shop and I have a five-year-old boy here asking if he can get a golf cart."

"I'll be right there," I said. I scrambled down to the local golf club which was about a quarter mile away.

Daniel and I had gone golfing a couple days prior for the first time. He loved riding in the cart and watching Dadda swing haphazardly at the little white ball. So, on this day, he decided he would go on his own. He proceeded to grab my best club and drag it for a quarter mile to the course. Yes, club head down, cement the whole way.

Upon arrival, he walked into the club house and told them we were here a couple days prior and that he wanted to get a cart and play.

Needless to say, they did not get him a cart. They asked for his phone number, so he gave it to them. They called and that is when we got the story download. So, we went down to get him.

Emergency contact

Whether your child is special needs or not, your kids need to have a way to contact you. Memorize your number, get them a medical bracelet, or something – anything. Moments like these can be scary for a parent. Knowing that he was prepared despite his behavior was relieving.

Relieved.

Year five was a big year for Daniel ... and us. We were finally able to get in to see a child neurologist and, after much effort to do so, were able to get an official diagnosis of high-functioning autism.

Granted, in 2002 that did not mean what it does today, but nevertheless its importance turned out to be huge over the course of his childhood.

I cannot understate the importance of getting an official diagnosis from a doctor. It is the key to getting any and all support from government-based entities (school, medical assistance, etc.)

Initially, the diagnosis allowed us to get IEPs (Individualized Educational Program) established at his school, which are basically agreements between the IEP members (his parents, teachers, special ed. admin, and others) on a custom plan for how to adapt his education for best effectiveness. But note that while this is documented and followed, *it is still up to you to advocate for your child*. Every necessary change is likely to be initiated by you. Every. Last. One.

Overwhelmed.

"In 2018–19, the number of students ages 3–21 who received special education services under the Individuals with Disabilities Education Act (IDEA) was 7.1 million, or 14 percent of all public-school students. Among students receiving special education services, 33 percent had specific learning disabilities," says the NCES[2]. Today, there are so many IEPs in schools that teachers are simply overwhelmed by the sheer number of "custom" efforts that must be made. They work to make this happen at every level, but I fear they are just overloaded and unable to really be successful due to that volume.

You are your child's best (and only) advocate. If you as the parent think something is not right, advocate for your child. No one else will. Ever. Pursue a diagnosis. Chase a resolution. Only you will be able to make it happen.

As time went on the diagnosis allowed us to apply and be approved for medical assistance. Eventually, this became a huge player in getting the support and therapy Daniel needed.

...from Daniel's sister...

My parents finally had enough and decided to take Daniel to a child neurologist. For the first time, they were able to get official documentation that something was wrong with Daniel. He was diagnosed with high-functioning autism, meaning that in day-to-day life, Daniel could behave and perform as a normal being, but with some certain things he seemed not to be as far along as others his age.

The diagnosis helped my parents show and explain to others that something was, in fact, different about Daniel, but it was frustratingly useless otherwise. In 2002, autism still was not very well-known or researched, and most people treated it the way they would someone with a hyperactive disorder. The schools, especially, just kind of shrugged it off, wrote up some kind of paperwork saying they were doing something about it, and moved on. Over the years, a continuous problem that my family faced was getting the support from the schools that Daniel needed to continue an education that was useful to him. Not until many, many years after diagnosis were we able to get Daniel what he needed, and even then, the school was still frustratingly unhelpful.

Get. The. Diagnosis.

This opens the door to therapy, medical assistance, custom education plans, and so much more. An example is medication. Now mind you, we were seriously concerned about putting him on meds. But we also knew he was chemically off-balance, and the goal was to give him a fighting chance in life. So, we worked with the doctors, therapists, and Daniel himself to understand what was working and what was not. All the time. This helped him have an optimal level of function so we could focus on the core issues while his body grew up.

The diagnosis will be the single most important step in raising a special needs child. Pursue it with everything you have. You know something is up. Convince them to do something about it.

Do it now.

Do not wait any longer.

It is too important.

---

[2] National Center for Education Statistics (NCES), "Students with Disabilities," May 2020, https://nces.ed.gov/programs/coe/indicator_cgg.asp (accessed December 8, 2020)

Age 6: A Slice of Expedition

> **Matthew 18:21-22 (MSG):**
>
> "At that point Peter got up the nerve to ask, "Master, how many times do I forgive a brother or sister who hurts me? Seven?" Jesus replied, "Seven! Hardly. Try seventy times seven."

Frustration.

One day, without our knowledge, Daniel grabbed a razor blade knife from my toolbox. You would think by now I would have figured out this should have been locked away, but we were never ones to "safety proof" our home, choosing rather to teach our children good choices and allow the natural consequences of bad choices to occur. Days (maybe even weeks) later I would find the third-row seat of my Expedition with a six-inch slice through the seat. On the good side, there was only one cut, but one is more than enough to a dad frustrated beyond belief at the lack of respect shown by his son.

Do not get me wrong, kids will be kids. They will spill milk at the table; they will walk through screen doors; and do many other things. But the overt destruction that began to surface, and stayed for many years to come, was likely one of the biggest struggles we faced over the long haul.

As mentioned previously, we bought a truck (our Expedition) to pull the trailer. We went well above our means to get this vehicle, recognizing that it, in combination with the trailer, would be replacing the house payment for the foreseeable future. In the end the truck lasted us 18 years and took us over 275,000 miles - a good choice in the long run. This was our first new vehicle and thus we committed to go big. We got everything we could for our money. This included leather seats throughout — a good choice given that we had young kids and that truck would be all they ever knew. Oh, the messes it saw! And well, the slice as well.

Hope for the best, plan for the worst

In the cat and mouse game of securing our home, I would never win. Daniel's creativity and ingenuity far exceeded my willingness to believe. In the end, I continually underestimated how far Daniel would go to get or do what he wanted. This would bite me over and over through the years and would create some very tense moments.

I always wanted to believe the best from him due to our teachings, but the reality was that he had only his self-interests in mind and was willing to do anything to get them.

Nevertheless, I trusted him repeatedly. He had the right baseline of values and principles and I believed he would overcome and never gave up on that belief. When we were tired, a new day appeared and gave us new strength.

Age 7: Dangling Displacement

Shocked.

"Hey! I'm sorry about the scratches on Daniel's forearms." These were the words we were welcomed with from our babysitter as we arrived home from a date night. "Um, ok. What happened?" She proceeded to explain that due to his behavior she locked Daniel in his room as we had suggested. After about fifteen minutes, she went up to check on him because it was very quiet. And when she opened the door, he was not there. She scrambled about to find where he went when she realized the window was wide open. Peering in was a vision of half a head (nose and up) and four fingers on each side as he hung out the second story window. She, of course, ran over and grabbed him by the arms, pulling him back through the window and apparently scratching his forearms on the brick in the process.

A little older from the last time he saw a long drop, but not much wiser, he hung outside over a brick veneer. Same house as previous, so once again, fifteen feet above the ground.

Whew.

I do not think we have ever been as thankful for a babysitter as then. She was truly amazing in handling the situation and we were ever appreciative of all those who were willing to take him on.

But we found out something that day we now call the "three-time babysitter rule." You see, by the time he was watched by a single person three times, he knew the buttons to push, edges to trim, and was always able to figure out the right manipulation paths to get his way. This is when we began to realize that his needs were well beyond autism. Because counter to anything an autistic child is, Daniel managed change well. He adapted. He improvised. He modified. In fact, much like his father, he thrived in change.

Prepare well

I cannot say enough for the time investment in getting a good babysitter. We got lucky – very lucky – as we were usually just appreciative to find someone willing to take him on at a rate we could afford. In many ways, we consider it much more than luck, as again it was the sovereignty of God in our lives. He is so much more capable than us. Our dependence on Him is so vital. And He takes care of His children.

Most special needs kids do not thrive in change like Daniel, so finding a couple of good and mature babysitters who understand your children and on whom you can rely is vitally important. The time and money you invest in this will pay off long-term more than you will ever know.

Restless.

After 9/11, along with many Americans, I had lost my job. Other than here-and-there work, as well as some good contracting work from a great friend, I was pretty much unemployed for two-plus years. I carried a pizza delivery job throughout just to keep the basics connected, but it was a very difficult time in the family. It was in 2004 when I finally got offered gainful employment, but it required a move to central California.

I grew up outside of Los Angeles, California. After the riots of 1992, I was pretty much done with living in that state. In no way did I ever intend to return. Nevertheless, it was a job, and so back we went.

Fresno had great people; I had a great job; we found a great church; and we truly created some great relationships. And it was even during this time that we found the value of mentorship — personally, and in marriage. We both found a couple of solid mentors and we were growing holistically in ways we had not experienced before.

Our kids adapted well to California and grew to love it. Every summer we had season passes to the water parks (because it is brutally hot in Central California) and the kids had settled into good school and church relationships.

But to be honest, Fresno was never a long-term placement for us. The weather and temperature, along with cultural differences, made it very difficult for us to assimilate, and we felt as if we never fit in. My wife and I both knew it and while we tried to make it work, it was the proverbial square peg in the round hole. Our quality of life was at an all-time low and no matter the trimming we would do, it would never fit ... and it would only hurt.

The impact of change

Moving. Again. We moved unusually often. Sometimes it was just a small move across town into a home that was more appropriate for our family. Sometimes it was in pursuit of my career as a software engineer. But many times, it came down to quality of life.

We consistently made choices that worked to improve overall life experience for the family. And often, that meant moving somewhere new.

As I thrive in change, this was simple. My wife thrived less in change, but very much in the opportunities on the horizon to improve her quality of life. And the kids? Well, kids are generally very adaptable. And ours had grown up with this type of change.

But know your kids.

The consideration of the impact of this type of change to a child with special needs is vital. Thankfully, we had come to learn that Daniel thrived in change. And our other two kids did fine with this as well – at least, until high school.

Age 8: Battle Royale

Frustrated.

At the airport: "Ok guys, I need to make sure you have nothing in your pockets before we go through security." Child #1 – check. Child #3 – check. Daniel – well... he proceeds to pull a pair of scissors out of his sweatshirt pocket.

I. Cannot. Even. I am so floored/stunned, I cannot even find any words. Scissors? Really? "WHY ON EARTH DO YOU HAVE SCISSORS IN THE AIRPORT?" I screamed in another moment of anger. He replied, "I wanted to cut stuff on the plane!" Stunned, I could only reply with "Um... OK... Well, please go throw those in the garbage thank you very much... Ugh."

We were headed out on vacation as a family and, of course, we *thought* we had appropriately handled all the logistics. After all, this was not our first ever trip - we all were familiar with travel and the process of getting through security checkpoints. And maybe that was the gripe more than anything. I guess a minor detail was missed in telling our kids that nothing can be in their pockets when going through security at an airport. I mean, I guess I am glad I caught it before reaching security as it could have been worse. Frustrating, nevertheless.

Scissors. Never had he before (and never has he since) ever carried scissors in his pockets. So random.

Communicate the plan

An innocent mistake? Perhaps. Although he did not have any paper, so I suppose what he was going to cut is anyone's guess.

But really this was more of a lesson for me in preparing my kids for the tasks of the day.

It reminds me of the story of the dad who took his daughter deer hunting and they set up separate stands. After some time, a beautiful deer with huge antlers came into perfect view and alongside him a smaller deer. His daughter waited ... and waited ... and waited. Dad was getting irritated when finally, BANG! And the little deer dropped. Perplexed, dad later asked why she shot the smaller one and she responded that she remembered she could only shoot a buck and so she waited until it reared up so she could confirm! Dad apparently forgot to mention that adult bucks have antlers.

Oops.

Communication is key.

Irritated.

It was during this time that we had another school transition. Due to our house not selling in Texas, we could no longer afford that house payment and the rent in California after about a year of trying. So, we pulled our travel trailer out of storage and decided that was the best option financially.

We ended up living in the trailer, as a family of five, in a not-so-great part of Fresno, California, for about six months. It was not an easy life, but it was the right choice for us.

Unfortunately, the move crossed us over (by one street) into a different school district (even if mid-year). At the time, we felt that the impact of a changing environment and school was not a preferred scenario for Daniel, so while we had to move to Fresno for job reasons, there was really no need to affect the kids for a simple move across town. We asked for a "transfer" (a document from the unified school district allowing a student to attend school in a different district) to stay in the current district for the remainder of the school year.

...from Daniel's sister...

Even while in the same state, we moved between homes, and even a camping trailer, more often than I can remember in the five-year span we spent there. It was difficult, but I was beginning to get used to it and was not too bothered by switching schools.

One move, however, had us being forced to switch schools in the middle of the year. Considering Daniel's difficulties with school already, changing the environment, courses, and peers was not a desirable situation. When my dad appealed for a transfer to stay in the same district until the end of the year, Daniel's was approved but mine was denied. I remember sitting in the living room listening to my parents talk about this, and I could tell my parents were upset. The concern was not necessarily me switching curriculum or courses, but the fact that I was Daniel's protector in school and there was worry for how he might be bullied if I were forced to leave.

Pride.

Then, out of the blue, my daughter had an idea. She suggested we challenge the district via a protest. I had never used that method before, so it came as a surprise, albeit a welcome one.

...from Daniel's sister (continued)...

Out of the blue, I thought of something without even realizing I had said it aloud. "What if I just stay?" My parents were kind of confused and stopped to ask what I meant. I had not fully formed the thought yet, so I remember speaking slowly as I considered it. I explained that I would continue to go to school, even though I was not supposed to. I figured they could not forcibly remove me (remember, I was ten) without causing serious problems for themselves, especially if other people found out about it.

Talk about putting pressure on us to make something happen. But I said, "Okay, if you are willing to do that, I will support you in every way I can." That day I sent a message to a few of the local media outlets advising them of what was going to ensue. And while most ignored my pleas for help, one stood out and did an interview with me. It turned out this investigative reporter was following up on multiple complaints with the district and was planning on doing a story within a couple of weeks anyway, so the timing was pretty good. After all was said and done, we were scheduled to be in front of the school that Friday, at the end of the school day, to protest the action.

In parallel I continued to attempt to resolve the issue through the district before our time was up. I had reached out directly to the superintendent and left a message to see if there were any last-minute changes that could happen. As Friday approached and my nerves were unraveling, there simply was no change in plan and the district was forcing me to transfer my kids to another school.

...from Daniel's sister (continued)...

Our solution, however, was not ideal, and I remember my dad telling me that he was still trying to talk to the district to get them to resolve the issue without having to resort to our plan. I remember being upset with him that he was still trying to give them a chance. They wanted to attack my family, fine! Let them have it! I was ready to brawl with the district. There is that stubbornness my mom gave me. In the end, my plan was unnecessary, but I still found my first lesson on just how little the school districts actually care about the well-being of their students.

Relieved.

Friday came and at about 10:00 AM I got a call from the superintendent's office that they would be allowed to stay. Needless to say, we were relieved, but now I had to scramble to get all the parallel plans cancelled out and somehow let our daughter know that her plans would be unnecessary.

I am thankful for a superintendent with a level head. Unfortunately, we later ran into other, even more substantial issues with the district staff.

Do right. And defend it.

Sometimes help comes from the most surprising places. Be open to it – you need all the help you can get in these scenarios. Our daughter's willingness to do the unexpected forced me to turn over rocks I might have otherwise not considered. Her stubbornness forced me to advocate for Daniel in new and creative ways. My daughter taught me to persevere, and truly she is still teaching me things today.

In addition, I learned the importance of supporting my child. Her willingness to step out and do something so in-the-face of authority established what would be a long-standing value for our family – **do what is right, because it is right.**

In the movie, "Letters to Iwo Jima," one of the young American soldiers dies in the custody of the Japanese. They pulled out a letter to his family and in it they read that his mom tells him to "do what's right, because it's right." In an epiphany moment, the Japanese soldier says that his mom tells him to do the same thing. Our daughter believed protecting her brother was right. And I believed in her.

Teach your kids values. And source them in fundamental moral principles. True morality comes from God and never changes. Godly principles stand the test of time and are not relative to situations.

Right principles stand through circumstance.

NOT vice versa.

Age 9: I Cannot See Anything

Stunned.

"Daddy, there's a lot of smoke in my room and I can't see anything." I scrambled upstairs and opened his door to find a complete fog – I literally could not see my hand in front of my face because it was so thick. There was no heat, however, so I was able to safely, but blindly, walk through to the window and opened it.

After the smoke dissipated, I was able to determine the source: a toy on the carpet and a handheld gas lighter that he was using to light said toy on fire. Fortunately, the only success he had was in lighting the flame-retardant carpet which just smoked considerably.

Whew!

Needless to say, we had to replace the carpet. And add smoke detectors ASAP as this could have been so much worse.

And another item identified to go into a secure place was the small gas lighter.

Every room in every house should have a functional smoke detector. I know that I am responsible for that – even in a rental. Do not depend on your previous owners or even your landlord. Do at least a basic assessment of your home and secure it appropriately. You, fathers, are responsible for the safety of your family. You and you alone.

My role as a father

It is my responsibility, as the father, to prepare my child to be a positive force in our world. It is my responsibility to teach them a strong work ethic, a solid set of values, a moral baseline, and principles which will turn him into a productive member of society. My role, as his father, is exactly that – to lead my child into who he needs to be as a man or woman. And that, irrespective of his "special needs." The Bible is clear that I will be held accountable for this, not my wife. And while she absolutely plays an incredibly important role in all the above, I am ultimately held responsible to lead.

From the moment of Daniel's diagnosis, we knew this task just got infinitely more difficult. But it was my task nonetheless, and one that I would not relinquish. We worked hard, incredibly hard, and at great expense, over his childhood to get him the support that he needed. We turned over rocks, looked behind proverbial walls, and dug up options that would help him get through the struggles he had. And we prayed often and hard (but never often enough or hard enough, I suppose).

In time, despite the doubts of many, the efforts prevailed.

Fathers, stepfathers, male guardians, etc.: I call you out today. And I call you up. The responsibility to lead your children (special needs or not) is yours and yours alone.

Be the man you need to be for your child. Train them. Grow them. It does not mean you do all the work (e.g., delegation of education to the school system is appropriate.) But YOU are responsible. You and you alone.

For those of you who do not have a father in the home, I encourage getting a father-figure to stand in the gap. Children need male role models – real men (not just males) that know what leadership means and can mentor that into the child's life. Similarly, there are fundamental characteristics that a child needs that can better be passed down from their mother – or a positive female role model. Both are necessary. If you are in a situation where only one parent is in play, please make sure to provide appropriate influences so your children can learn and understand the positive influences of both honorable femininity and masculinity.

And, as I mentioned for ourselves, it is always beneficial to have mentor relationships in our lives - as adults, and as children. You should initiate that into their lives so that it becomes second nature.

Alarmed

"Daddy, I filled your tank up for you on the truck!" he yelled in pride!

"Um," as I looked outside in horror to see the garden hose in the truck's gas tank.

Another trip to the shop and some hundreds later, we were back to normal. Ugh.

Mischievous vs. devious

Some kids are just mischievous. And some are not. We tend to measure the "goodness" of our children based on this. But the reality is some naturally push the borders and boundaries where others are content living well within them.

Start by giving your kids a baseline of values and principles. This usually starts at a young age and might even be reactive initially but the sooner you can get in front of situations, the better. And when you define the boundary, if possible, back it out to a value or principle that can be applied irrespective of circumstance. An example would be truth. There is no circumstance where lying is okay. It might seem to have short-term benefit, but the long-term impact will always outweigh it. Truth is a deep character value – and lying is a deep character flaw.

Then, realize that consistency in application is vital. Walk the talk: If your kids see you violating the rules you established, they will ignore them. If one kid sees you being more lenient toward her brother, she will see it and question it.

And finally, judge (and discipline) based on their actions, but be considerate of their intentions. As expensive as it was, his heart was in the right place when filling my gas tank with water. The discipline for his actions still needed to occur, but not to the extent of burning his toys where the action was both dangerous and with ill intent.

Age 10: Brain Games

"After 35 years of being a child neurologist, I've never quite seen a kid like Daniel," said his neurologist. In essence, his summary was that Daniel ebbs and flows through all aspects of the special needs' spectrum. Whether it be autism, ADD (Attention Deficit Disorder), ADHD (Attention Hyperactivity Deficit Disorder), OCD (Obsessive Compulsive Disorder), ODD (Oppositional Defiance Disorder), APD/SPD (Auditory / Sensory Processing Disorder), bi-polar, PDD (Pervasive Development Disorder), or others, Daniel will change and adapt each day based on a myriad of reasons (which we continue not to understand).

…from Daniel's sister…

One of his struggles that affected my family most deeply was his symptoms of bipolarity. One moment, he would be joking and laughing with the family, and then an off handed or misplaced comment would send Daniel into a fit of rage. As he got older and began expressing his anger violently, he became dangerous. Our family was forced to be hypersensitive and on our toes 24/7, causing everyone's stress level to increase dramatically. And, just like a circle, our stress could only be contained for so long before it was expressed, which in turn would set Daniel off. It was a never-ending cycle, and unfortunately, to this day still has not been completely resolved.

In short, change became the norm for our "autistic" kid, and it was the first time that autism became a non-focus, and we began to embrace adaptation – the change he was embracing daily.

For myself, this was not difficult. I thrive in change. I have learned to adapt and to be flexible. Most importantly, I have learned that depending on Christ for direction in my life means truly letting him "direct my paths." This one learning is so deep and based in so much Biblical truth, that I encourage you to dive in and research it. Suffice it to say, it is the essence of why "prayer without ceasing" is so vital to the Christian life. Proverbs 16:9 (MSG) says, "We plan the way we want to live, but only God makes us able to live it."

...from Daniel's sister (continued)...

Unlike many other autistic children, Daniel's ADHD tendencies meant he could never deal with a strict schedule. Having every moment of the day planned out, exactly the same as every other day, was never something he could deal with. If there was not variety in there, he would freak out. Even something as simple as a daily schedule at school was always a struggle for him. He would get bored, distracted, and move on to do something else, even if he knew he would get in trouble for doing so. Daniel cannot do schedules, plans, or anything remotely regimented. Sometimes it is a curse, and other times, a blessing. At least we can rest assured that he will rarely be bored.

Never being okay with the clear (to us) issues Daniel was facing, we continually pursued support, help, guidance, etc.

...from Daniel's sister (continued)...

For someone like me, who loves plans, schedules, organization, and anything else in that category, living with Daniel's spontaneity was often aggravating. My mom would tell me the things we would be doing for the day, and even as a young girl, I would automatically start segmenting the day into those different activities. Then along came Daniel, changing plans last-minute and altering the day's schedule according to his desires and sudden attitude changes. It would irritate me so much that I would get into arguments with my family whenever it happened, just because *my* plan was being changed.

This has always been a struggle for me, and even today, it still gets to me whenever I visit with a plan in mind and Daniel (or anyone else) just wrecks it. This innate need of mine to schedule and plan things has always been a point of tension in my relationships, but even more so with God, and it is something I am still working through to this day.

When he was ten, we found a child neurologist locally who would help us to address some of the continuing issues we were seeing both in fine motor skills and in the growing behavioral problems.

As we learned about the traits of autism, we came to understand that at the appropriate times in the growth process, the synapses of the brain do not connect at the rate expected.

"Brain Games" was a program developed to help people connect those synapses. Daniel's involvement in this program allowed him to begin to understand the *whys* around his actions. More importantly, it helped us to begin to understand more specifics around his needs.

The reality was that Daniel would be special needs and we would never have a day where we could rely on a schedule, a process, or a way of working – because it would change ... every ... single... day.

Hopeless.

As a parent this is a hard realization. I think it was at this point when Mama began to accept the scenario that Daniel may never be ready for the real world on his own and that he would spend the rest of his life at home. What a place to find ourselves. I mean, really no parent ever wants to face "beyond normal" difficulties. Whether it be the death of a child, daily struggles of physical disabilities, or even the prospect of growing a child through mental disabilities. However, many must accept the realization early on that their child will need help forever.

I applaud those parents who not only recognize this and process through it, but step up, own it, and continue to work with their child with hope for the future. You will be your child's hero – even though they may never recognize it or be able to express it. And if they do not, you are a hero to many of us who understand the struggle and recognize the hell that you must go through daily. Your child deserves your hope. Please do not give up.

You were made for this

As a Christian, I fundamentally believe that God's sovereign hand guided us to live in places where we would get the right help for our child at the right time of his life. We continually ran into solutions for our child that happen to be in the areas where we lived, even though we raised him in a time where the issues were not well understood, and help was not readily available.

Today, there are people who can likely help you. But even if you cannot find local help, do not let location be a barrier for you. God placed this child in your hands because he knew you would be the best parents for him. Be that. And do whatever it takes.

Whenever you struggle, remember this: God does not make mistakes. We naturally question ourselves as being capable to handle the burden placed on us. God puts us in many situations that are beyond our strength; for the purpose of us leaning into Him for His strength. But in our doubts, remember this, God does not make mistakes.

YOU are the BEST parent for your child. AND, that child is the best child for you too. You will learn and grow in ways you might never have had an opportunity otherwise. I may not be the best dad in the world, but I am absolutely the best dad for Daniel (and the other kids). But more importantly, the corollary is that they are the best kids for me – and I will be a better person for them recognizing that I was placed here on this earth as their parent: to love them; to raise them; and to prepare them to be productive members of society. No one can do that like I can ... for them.

Age 11: And the Damage Begins

Hebrews 12:7-11 (MSG):

"My dear child, don't shrug off God's discipline, but don't be crushed by it either. It's the child he loves that he disciplines; the child he embraces, he also corrects. God is educating you; that's why you must never drop out. He's treating you as dear children. This trouble you're in isn't punishment; it's training, the normal experience of children. Only irresponsible parents leave children to fend for themselves. Would you prefer an irresponsible God? We respect our own parents for training and not spoiling us, so why not embrace God's training so we can truly live? While we were children, our parents did what seemed best to them. But God is doing what is best for us, training us to live God's holy best. At the time, discipline isn't much fun. It always feels like it's going against the grain. Later, of course, it pays off handsomely, for it's the well-trained who find themselves mature in their relationship with God."

Torn.

It was about this time that the struggle we were having with our quality of life in Fresno began to come to a head. That, along with frustrations at work, had us all on edge. When Daniel turned eleven, I was offered a job in Pennsylvania and we jumped at the opportunity to get out of Fresno.

Daniel's sister had just started high school at an incredible school in California, so this move could not have come at a worse time. This was the first time in all our moves where the kids seemed to really get hit hard by it. And it was this time, after 17 moves in 17 years, we decided it needed to stop. To this day, we feel guilty for making the move but knew it was the right move for us at the right time. But this time my wife and I committed to make it work.

...from Daniel's sister...

The move to Pennsylvania was probably one of the hardest difficulties I faced in my life up to that point. I was not happy with my parents' decision, and they knew it. Looking back, I know I was hard on them and I only made things more difficult. But when you are in the middle of your Freshman year of high school and looking at moving across the country to a place where you do not know the people or the culture, suddenly things look very bleak.

At the time, the move to Pennsylvania was devastating to me and caused my first serious bout of depression. But as the years progressed and I made friends, we found a church I liked, and I ended up finding a place where things just fit for me. I fell in love with the state of Pennsylvania. I love the rolling hills, the orchards, the Amish farms. I love the smell of cow manure and food factories. I love the small, local shops you can find in the downtown areas around the state. I loved my church, and I developed a stronger bond with God because of the struggles I faced during that transition. In the end, what I thought would be the end of the world actually ended up being the beginning of it. The experiences I went through would end up being defining moments of my life. I thank God that He encouraged my parents to make that decision, despite my insistence otherwise.

In the end, the support Daniel ended up getting here in PA was amazing, so we know it was worth it. But our daughter took the hit on this one, and it was something we could never really give back to her. She struggled adapting to the new high school and never really felt like she fit in.

...from Daniel's sister (continued)...

Dealing with Daniel's issues during this time was not on my radar, and it showed. I became indifferent to him and to the family; continually focused on my own needs in transitioning to the new school, the new culture, and everything else.

But during this time my focus on my own issues meant I became less tolerant of Daniel and all his antics. As his behaviors and reactions varied, mine became more concrete. He would say or do something, I would immediately be irritated. As I grew older and watched the violence both with Daniel and my dad escalate, I began to get more involved. I started to spiral into a routine pattern that was devastating, both to myself and to the rest of my family. Anger became a constant norm in our house, and the three of us became an ever-boiling cauldron of tension and emotion.

Annoyed.

It was around this time that Daniel was transitioning into a teenager and his hormones were beginning to throw a new mix into his already messed up mental world. As would be expected, his ability to manage this was exactly like his dad — uncontrolled anger. For Daniel, this manifested itself physically — from throwing game controllers through the TV to hitting walls (and breaking through them). Nothing he had not seen me do over the years.

That year we did a lot of drywall patching. And soon Daniel began to understand the consequences of his actions as I taught him to fix things around the house. If he hit the wall, he fixed the wall. No, the quality of the work was not good, but he paid the price anyway. And sometime later I would come along and fix it properly.

Additionally, if Daniel began to get angry, he had to agree to go to his room and we would lock him in. This was really when his room began to take a beating.

In time, Daniel's mind began to understand that walls were not too difficult to bust through. One day, after being locked in his room, he showed up downstairs and asked us a question. Surprised not by the question but by his presence, we of course had to ask. Well, we found out that he had beat a hole into his wall, and then also into the wall of his brother's room. Then he proceeded to climb through.

One might be wondering how we did not hear this. Well, the sound of him beating on the wall was a very normal occurrence, so we would not have noticed any significant difference.

Little did we know, but this lesson would be learned again and again: if he wants out (or in) he will use whatever means necessary to get his way.

Needless to say, that was a substantial repair to deal with. In this case, I decided we would "Daniel-proof" his room. He and I ripped out all the drywall from his room and placed a piece of thin plywood on all the walls. Then we proceeded to replace the drywall on top. This made a barrier that he would forever be unable to penetrate - though that certainly did not stop him from trying.

But, when the walls do not budge, find something that does. At one point in a fit of rage he kicked out the glass in his window. As you can imagine, that did not turn out too well. The shatter caused me to run upstairs where I found him sitting out on the patio roof with a trail of blood leading from the window to him.

We ended up in the hospital where he was gifted with a substantial set of stitches in his foot. Suffice it to say, the window replacement was with tempered glass to ensure safety in the future.

At 11 years old Daniel was very aware of our behavioral expectations and his (and equally my) anger were not okay behaviors. But these incidents had become so common that our responses had literally been reduced to "what now?" We never knew what was next, but we reacted and addressed every scenario in a way that would keep him safer and minimize risk moving forward. All the while, we would continue to try and address the core issues that were triggering his anger.

Eventually, this cycle of anger and our attempt to keep him safe removed just about everything Daniel had in his room except his mattress.

This was difficult because we wanted to provide him with good and enjoyable things, but he continually behaved in a disrespectful fashion and thus removed himself from the privilege of having nice things.

Kids need discipline.

What that means to everyone is different, but the simple fact is that kids need (and want) boundaries (but will never tell you so). But boundaries mean nothing if there are no consequences when those boundaries are crossed. How you implement those consequences are yours to work through, but not providing them with consequences will be teaching them counter to the way the real-world works. In our kids' case, we established early that "their" possessions were blessings — privileges to enjoy. It was important for them to know that their blessings could also be taken away as a consequence of bad behaviors. Daniel pushed this limit to the extent of having almost everything taken from him. And he would cycle through getting something back and then losing it again.

Without consequences, they will have no understanding of the importance of moral and ethical values, the impact of hard work, and a myriad of other positive life lessons. Teach them boundaries; and give them consequences. They will not like it, but they will learn to understand it — and in the end, will appreciate and love you for teaching them how to be productive members of society.

*You are **not** their friend - you are their **parent**. You are there to prepare them for the real world — and it is the PRIMARY responsibility you have with your kids.*

Age 12: Help

Impatient.

A six-month waiting list? For what? My wife had connected to a local facility called Philhaven CADD (Center for Autism Developmental Disorders) in our new home of Pennsylvania. Having recently moved across the country and taken on a new opportunity, we began working through getting settled. Philhaven would come to be a multi-dimensional support facility for Daniel's very dynamic needs. This facility had multiple locations focused on different aspects of the spectrum, including both inpatient and outpatient services depending on the behavioral and safety needs of the situation. And as said previously, it really was a Godsend to us, though we really would not know how much or to what extent at this time.

Six months later Daniel was accepted into the program. The process was initially very slow. A psychologist was assigned to begin assessing his needs and eventually that turned into acceptance into the after-school program that he ended up attending for a few years. They worked on his socialization and behavioral issues specifically.

In time, the support services also included a TSS (Therapeutic Support Specialist) visiting three times a week for an hour, and then it graduated into more extensive family therapy options where we had different teams (over time) of therapists assigned to us for different therapy needs throughout the week (usually one hour with Daniel, one hour with the family unit, and one hour with just the parents). This holistic approach allowed us to continually address his dynamically changing needs and work through issues as they arose.

And as his anger was the clear frontrunner of issues we needed to address, the Philhaven therapists implemented a safety plan for the family. Supporting the reversed door locks, Daniel would be sent to his room to self-manage. Similarly, all of us had plans to go to our rooms and lock the doors if we were not able to get Daniel to his. And finally, if we were not able to get to our rooms, we exited the house for protection; and if Daniel were outside (as was the case a few times), we would lock the doors of the house barring entry until he self-managed and calmed down.

As we look back, Philhaven was truly a Godsend. We are incredibly thankful to have such a world-class facility local to us to help us through the troubling times that were to come. The safety plans were brilliant in protecting all of us, including Daniel.

Have a safety plan

I cannot imagine what life would have been like without the safety plan. And while we had multiple reasons for implementing it, it reminded me of an extension of my original one — the whistle. We need things in our lives that address emergency scenarios for safety and security.

We do this (or should) for fires, earthquakes, hurricanes, etc. We might even have a first aid kit handy. It is smart to be prepared. And the more things that could potentially go awry, the more you should be prepared with a plan.

Take the time to assess your life and the things you should be putting in place to protect your family. And do not forget life insurance, a will, and a health directive (this outlines your preferences for your future healthcare in case you are deemed incapable of making decisions on your own).

For quite some time we had a simple rule with the kids: you can be in two formal activities outside of school ... and one must be church. A spiritual foundation is the most important thing for us to teach our children and we would drive this as being an integral part of everything they did.

But the second was their choice. Daniel tried football but did not have the perseverance. He tried a couple other things as well, but what seemed to stick with all three of our kids was Judo.

We were introduced to it from a co-worker and black belt. Judo is a martial art and sport adapted from jujitsu, which uses principles of balance and leverage. What sets it aside from other forms of martial arts is that it is a defensive form of self-protection. This mentality (of defensive versus offensive) ended up being critical in shaping the way our kids viewed and utilized it.

They all started at the same time and we would go once or twice a week to learn the basics of this sport. As parents, we were very excited that they seemed to enjoy this – especially since they were all together and it made getting them to and from their activities simple and straightforward. In the beginning, I even joined with them (until I was later injured).

All three kids grew in success similarly along the way. We loved the self-discipline it was teaching them and appreciated that they had something alongside school on which they could focus. Every six months we would go to promotional events and competitions, and they were consistently moving up in their ranks.

...from Daniel's brother...

I remember Dad taking us to Judo early on, but it really was not something I enjoyed. Our dojo was in an old barn and there was no central heat / air so in the winter I was always really cold and, in the summer, it was too hot for me to enjoy. Additionally, there were too many people for me to get the personal attention that I preferred.

Eventually I found a good sparring partner and we began to really support each other. I got good enough to be able to start teaching others and that also really gave me strong personal encouragement in the sport.

Every now and then, however, I would be matched against Daniel. Early on this was not a problem, but as his anger grew, it was primarily directed toward our family. This came full force during our matches when, practice or not, Daniel would be overly aggressive and even threatening. I felt he always had something to prove and I was his target.

To me it always seemed like Daniel used Judo to get his anger out, instead of really using it to learn discipline.

There were times the kids did not want to go. For these times, we had to find the motivators. For Daniel, it was money. I divided the amount we paid each month by the number of practices and said if he chose not to go then he had to pay for that session. This at least motivated him to go. There were a few times he just sat on the sideline, but any competitor knows it is extra difficult to watch someone play your sport while you are on the sideline. We just allowed him to work through that in his own mind.

...from Daniel's sister...

Judo was a powerful tool for my brothers and me. I am a strong believer that self-defense is a critical lesson every child should be taught. While it took each of us different amounts of time and motivation to really click with it, it ended up being one of the most beneficial things we could have done with our time.

Unfortunately, Daniel could never figure out how to separate our home life from the dojo, and so we would often find ourselves the target of his anger even in what was supposed to be a safe place. There were many times where the dojo was filled with three age groups: adults, young children, and then us three siblings. This caused us to be sparring partners more often than not, which contributed to much of the hesitation my youngest brother and I felt when it came to participating. Daniel did not understand the basic concepts of balance and looseness, often choosing instead to come to the mat with aggression and violence.

Daniel got pretty good at Judo and would be involved for quite a few years to come. He had opportunities to do demonstrations both at school and in church and this really boosted his morale.

Extra-curricular activities

Your kids should be involved in extra-curricular activities beyond TV and video games. But just as everything in life should have a balance, they need you to be the example of that balance – in your life and in how you raise them. We consistently assess the value of time in our lives and where we invest it, continually adjusting to ensure the right priorities and the right commitment. After all, there are many more good things in this world than you have time in which to commit. So, balance it. Establish the one-to-two priorities in your life that will fulfill you and teach your children to do the same. Every business can survive "with or without you" so do what's right for you.

Lonely.

As my wife was beginning to isolate herself from Daniel, it was around this time that our daughter began to form a Mom-complex. As she watched Daniel act and behave in certain ways (usually I was at work), she would grow frustrated that her mom would not do what she thought she should. She would not yell at Daniel, she would not punish him for saying inappropriate things, she would hardly interact with him whenever he would go off the deep end. Our daughter began to get so frustrated with her mom that she started to feel it was her responsibility to step in. If mom was not going to punish him, then she would. And this way of thinking led to very dangerous territory.

> *...from Daniel's sister (continued)...*
>
> Daniel would do something, and I would immediately react. He would get frustrated with the video games and throw the controller; I would grab it and not give it back to him. Enter: anger. My mom would tell him to do something and he would not do it; I would step in and yell at him to do it, oftentimes repeatedly. Enter: anger. He would break something in the house; I would yell at him to fix it. Enter: anger.

Our daughter eventually came to see herself not only as a stand-in mom, but as the protector whenever I was not home. Anytime Daniel threatened to or did harm someone, she saw it as her responsibility not only to stop it, but to ensure it did not happen again. By whatever means necessary. For a long time, our daughter did not understand that Daniel simply could not fathom how that process worked. So, their endless arguments and fistfights just circled around again and again, causing more pain and stress for the family.

> *...from Daniel's sister (continued)...*
>
> As he grew older and stronger, things began escalating further, and so did I. He would get mad at the dogs for some reason, start beating on them or kicking them. So, I would turn around and do the same thing to him. This was a process that was repeated more often than I care to admit. Objects, pets, people. Whatever he hit, I repaid him for it. My anger turned to violence, and instead of one dangerous person in the house, there became two.

It was then that Philhaven came through again, this time with family services. From here we met with a team of therapists at least three times per week: one was with the whole family; one was with just my wife and me; and then one was continuing the TSS service that Daniel had meeting with him at least once per week with direct support.

...from Daniel's sister (continued)...

My instincts of self-preservation and family protection began to turn into a savage and uncontrollable thing. Something would spark Daniel's anger, and he would start raging. I could feel the heat in my own body rise as he started throwing things and yelling at the rest of us. It eventually got to the point where he did not even need to touch or hurt someone for me to go into mother-bear mode; I was already there (but less of a mother bear and more of a wild wolf).

This process continued for years and I began to resent Daniel, and eventually I grew to hate him. It is a place that I hated being in, but it was where I found myself for a long time. I hated having him around and I hated having to admit that he was my brother. But deep down, I hated myself for not being able to maintain control whenever I was around him.

Sibling rivalries

The interplay between my Daniel and his sister was not healthy. And the pent-up anger our daughter harbored was quite dangerous. And not something to which mom and I really saw the extent. It was great that the family counseling came into play, but I fear it was all a bit too late. By that time, his sister had lost all desire to resolve this conflict. And it has unfortunately scarred her even to this day.

Parents - be engaged in the interaction with your children. We all understand sibling rivalry but prepare yourselves so that you can recognize when it goes too far and address it immediately. The long-term impact is so much worse than the effects of the immediate action.

I beg of you – be prepared for this. Your children have the potential of being the greatest of lifetime friends – or equally the greatest of enemies.

Age 13: Fear

> **Romans 8:28 (MSG):**
>
> "Meanwhile, the moment we get tired in the waiting, God's Spirit is right alongside helping us along. If we don't know how or what to pray, it doesn't matter. He does our praying in and for us, making prayer out of our wordless sighs, our aching groans. He knows us far better than we know ourselves, knows our pregnant condition, and keeps us present before God. That's why we can be so sure that every detail in our lives of love for God is worked into something good."

Terrified.

"Daddy! Daniel is coming through the door with an axe! Help! What should I do?" said our daughter in frantic concern. I ran out of the office, jumped in the car, and screamed home, keeping her on the phone as I drove. Oh, the thoughts running through my head: of course, fear for the safety of my other kids; concern over the intentions of Daniel; etc. But the last thing on my mind was getting stopped for speeding or any other thing that could have happened on the way home – I was hell bent to arrive at the house and it did not matter who might have followed.

I asked her to explain what was happening and basically, she was concerned about his anger, so she implemented our safety plan and locked the doors to the house while he was in the garage. Little did I know that his sister secretly began using that as a tactic that would trigger him.

...from Daniel's sister...

As Daniel's anger and violence continued to evolve, our family went through a variety of safety plans. At some point, Daniel started forming a habit of leaving the house whenever he found himself getting angry (I believe this was a plan implemented by himself and one of his counselors at the time). I, being the hateful sister that I was, would proceed to run around the house locking every possible entrance back in. The first few times I always managed to miss one, like the basement door or one of the ground-floor windows. But eventually I got the hang of it. Sure, it would aggravate Daniel more and eliminate the progress he was making with removing himself from the situation. But I did not understand that. And frankly, I did not really care about him anymore.

When he realized the door was locked and wanted to get back in, he proceeded to go to the shed and grab the axe and began hacking down the steel door separating the garage from the house!

...from Daniel's brother...

It was winter and quite cold outside, but Daniel's sister would not let that stop her from locking Daniel out when "appropriate." Her animosity towards Daniel was so strong that anything she could do to rid herself of him was ok.

Something happened (this was common) that caused Daniel's anger to start escalating, so he went outside to avoid the situation. Upon doing so, his sister locked all the doors in the house just to antagonize him. Eventually he got cold and began banging on the door-to-the-garage to let him in the house. We continued to ignore him.

And then BANG! An incredibly loud noise emanated from the garage. We were sitting in the kitchen adjacent to the door and, as our eyes were fixed on the door, we again heard a BANG! This time, though, we saw the axe head come through the steel door.

It was then we started to panic.

The other kids scrambled to our daughter's room, locked the door, and then called me. I suggested they run down and out the front door and get out of the house entirely, but fear had taken over, and they were cowering upstairs in her room.

...from Daniel's sister (continued)...

I served seven and a half years in the military, and I have still never felt so afraid in my life. My first thought was to call the police, but I had always recognized how serious police calls could get, so I chose to call Dad first. I do not remember everything that he said, but I do remember him telling me to grab my younger brother, run upstairs to my room, and lock the door. He told me not to say a word to Daniel, not to be loud or make any sounds, and to wait for Dad because he was on his way.

Helpless.

As I sped home, Daniel continued to swing, shredding the door that he was attempting to get through. Eventually a couple well-placed shots on the doorknob rendered it no longer effective and he was able to gain entry.

As mentioned previously, when he wants something, he will do anything to get it. Fortunately, in this case, he simply wanted access into the house. So, he did what he had to do to get it.

Then he simply proceeded to put the axe away, walk in, grab some chips, sit down, and watch TV. All the while the other kids are scared for their lives upstairs.

I got home and, needless to say, a rousing rendition of arguments ensued. It was then I escalated, per Philhaven's safety plan, to get him put into the Mt. Gretna hospital.

Mt. Gretna is a Philhaven facility that is a short-term in-placement facility to address escalated behavioral or safety concerns – clearly something for which Daniel qualified based on his actions. He spent two weeks there on this trip – focused entirely on his anger and addressing how he responds to various situations in life. Most importantly, understanding the impact of his extremism on his family. This was really his first time being away from family for an extended time and thus, while we visited often, the impact was high and beneficial.

...from Daniel's sister (continued)...

That incident was the first time that his violence had escalated to something so dramatic, and the first time we were able to convince anybody that weekly counseling sessions were not enough. We were able to get him into a "hospital", which was more of a live-in counseling center, and his first session lasted about two weeks. It was useful for him, and I think the first time he really began to understand his impact on our family, but it would definitely not be his last visit there.

When God matters most

What is your backup plan? What happens if something entirely out of your control happens to your kids? We can have the best laid plans that lie in ruins due to unforeseen circumstances. For us, an utter dependence on God and His omnipotent plan is reassuring beyond anything we can have on this earth.

The book (and movie) "The Shack"³ lays this out so well. I would challenge you to read / watch this. In short, it is not God that causes bad things to happen in our lives. That is the consequences of free will and evil influence. But it absolutely is God that is working through all the circumstances for the good of those that love Him. And it is good as He sees it – not as we see it.

If you are struggling through something, ask for His perspective – not for your solution.

It was also at this time that I had the opportunity to pursue an international assignment with my company ... in China. My career had transitioned from being a software engineer into management and now I was being groomed for the next steps in my career and a growth path that was increasingly fast. I felt blessed to be in a place where I was appreciated for the value I could bring to the table and it really looked like the company was ready to invest in my future.

Disappointment.

As my wife and I contemplated the possibility of moving to an unknown country, the only barrier we could find was Daniel.

But that was a big barrier. Daniel was getting amazing support – something we had spent the last 13 years pursuing. And yet, I was in that pivotal moment in my career where the trajectory was rapidly positive.

But deep down we knew what needed to be done. Because of the support that he was getting locally, we knew we could not leave. Our priority is what is best for the family, not for me. My time would come, but it was not now.

It was a very difficult day when I walked into my boss's office to let him know I had to stay. Thankfully, he had a huge heart and completely understood my plight.

It was a tough decision – one I would repeat again if I necessary. But one that would ultimately remove the opportunity for future growth within that company.

Priorities

Much like the prioritization of your spouse over your children, prioritizing your family over your job, your friends, etc. is also important.

I do not regret in anyway the decision to choose my son. But honestly, the decision could have been much worse – I might have been put in a situation where I would lose my job. I am thankful that was not the case, but you should prepare yourself for this type of scenario.

What would you do if ...? Worrying about the future is not healthy but planning for it is.

"Hope for the best, plan for the worst." Alternatively, consider this, "What a God! His road stretches straight and smooth. Every God-direction is road-tested. Everyone who runs toward him makes it." — Psalm 18:30 (MSG)

---

[3] William P. Young, *The Shack,* (Windblown Media, July 1, 2007)

Age 14: Over and Over Again

Exhausted.

January - Mt. Gretna. February – Mt. Gretna. March – Mt. Gretna. The cycle repeated over and over. We got a break for a few months and then it happened again. Then we seemed to have a good stretch until near the end of the year when it happened one more time.

Every time, anger. Every time, some behavioral trigger that sent him down a rabbit hole needing support beyond that which his family could provide.

...from Daniel's sister...

During my junior and senior years in high school, I delved into a very dark place. I became easily angered and violent,

I had no patience, and the kindness that I once so easily embraced had disappeared.

Hate became a norm for me. I eventually began admitting to people that I did hate my brother, starting with my friends, and sooner or later having the conversation with my parents. I remember hearing from my mother quite often phrases like "hate is a strong word" and "oh, you can't hate him, he's your brother!" To this day, though, I know that, unfortunately, hate really was what I felt for Daniel. Thinking back on those years, I now have feelings of shame and regret, but at the time, I could not fathom anything like what normal siblings were supposed to feel.

Incompetence.

Oh, the feelings of inadequacy. To know that no matter how hard we tried, we were failing. But also knowing that God was working through this, using support from external sources, to help get us through.

...from sister (continued)...

Riding along with my anger and hate was fear. I was absolutely afraid of Daniel. I was afraid of what he could do to myself and others. I was afraid of what he might become if he continued following a downward spiral. As Daniel first began exploring his anger through violence, his focus was usually on objects: game and TV controllers, walls, doors. This alone was enough to give us all a good scare. But as he got into his teen years and his hormones started raging (while mine were also in a similar process), his focus started to change in an ugly way, and he began to take out his frustrations on living things.

One day Daniel went into a fit of rage outside of the garage. Just due to the circumstances, I had an urge to shield him. Not having any method to the madness, I ran to him and did a full-body squeeze locking his arms and holding him tight. I had never hugged Daniel in this way, so it spooked me a bit. My impetus was protection. Protection for him. But also, protection from him.

I found out later that it was an appropriate form of handling the situation as the sensory hold from his father was comforting, even if constricting. In fact, it is not unlike the idea of a weighted blanket, which is often used for sensory kids. It is the same feeling you get when you are getting an x-ray on a table and they put a lead apron on you to eliminate the x-ray from affecting other areas of your body. That weight is comforting.

Comfort

In the movie, The Accountant[4], a scene drew up some memories that I would have rather forgotten. The main character deals with a high-functioning form of autism (not unlike Daniel in some ways, but every kid is different enough that you should not categorize.) As a young kid, his father and mother disagree on how to raise him and the mother decides she cannot handle it, so she leaves. In an extended fit of rage, the kid begins destroying things. The dad (who for the most part is an enabler for some horrible long-term behavioral issues in his child) runs through the house and grabs his son, holding him tightly.

Protection is our job as parents. Sometimes that takes methods that are uncomfortable or approaches that are perhaps different. Be willing to step out into the unknown and do what is best for your children.

This was also the year he tried his hand at stealing. Granted, his compulsion for food created this problem as, despite our best efforts, he would steal food consistently and hide it in his room. This ultimately led to us locking the pantry and freezer in ways that were *almost* fool proof. But this time he went outside the home and were it not for the grace of our neighbor, would have likely landed him in jail.

Disillusioned.

One day we found a couple of Tonka-like trucks in the garage – ones I knew were not ours. Trying to dig into where these came from, he always rationalized in a reasonable way. "The neighbor kid gave them to me," he said. That almost ended it, but then later I found another one in a different location causing me to pause as something did not feel right.

I asked Daniel to grab the toys and walk with me to the neighbor's house. I proceeded to ask if their kids had given the toys to Daniel and, to my surprise, the answer was no. More importantly, was the ensuing conversation. Not only were they not given to him, but the toys had also come from inside their house. This rightly "set off" our neighbor and she proceeded to give Daniel quite the lecture. As he deserved every bit of it, I let it continue not interrupting or defending him, recognizing it to be good for them both.

At the end, she threatened to call the police if it ever happened again. He apologized and agreed not to do it again. As far as I know, he never did. I always appreciated her standing her ground that his actions were not okay. But I also appreciated her grace, in not forcing the issue directly to law enforcement. His lesson was learned, and the second chance was appropriate.

Grace

The most common definition I have heard for grace is undeserved merit – or favor given to someone despite their not deserving it. While my neighbor was a great example of this, there is one greater. The sacrifice that Jesus made on the cross by sacrificing His life for ours is the ultimate example of grace. He paid for our sins, forever, with that one completely selfless act.

---

[4] *The Accountant*, DVD, Directed by Gavin O'Connor, Burbank: Warner Bros. Pictures, 2016

Age 15: Suicidal Living

> **Proverbs 25:11-12 (MSG):**
>
> *"The right word at the right time is like a custom-made piece of jewelry, And a wise friend's timely reprimand is like a gold ring slipped on your finger."*

Walking into my room I saw Daniel sitting down next to bed where mama lie, in his hand a 12" kitchen knife. "Umm, what are you doing?" I said (calm on the exterior but freaking out internally). "I don't want to be here anymore," he said.

Scared.

Fully afraid for my wife and myself as well as Daniel having no idea of his intent at the time, I proceeded to "talk him down" and got the knife away. But that again triggered a safety response plan.

In this case, Daniel was admitted to a long-term support facility. Reasonably local (within 2 hours away), Hoffman Homes became his home for the next six months. The focus? Safety.

As we were admitting him, it became clear they would not address behavioral concerns, but rather focused on safety. This was somewhat frustrating, but we understood and accepted the plan. Behavioral concerns, such as his anger issues, were not going to be directly addressed. The focus of Hoffman was addressing his and others' safety in the context of daily life.

...from Daniel's sister...

Daniel's anger did not get better or worse, but his understanding of its impact on the family finally hit home. And it hit him hard.

My parents became scared that he would harm himself. Instead of saying "I hate you", he began to say things like "I hate myself" and "I wish I weren't like this". It eventually got to the point where my parents had to get him admitted somewhere that he would be safer. However, this would not be the same short-term location he had already been in and out of for quite a few months.

My parents got him into a program where he would live in a location approximately 2 hours away and, for all intents and purposes, live in a college-like setting (but much more structured). He lived in a small building like a dorm, which he shared with other kids his age who were struggling with similar issues.

He lived there for a few months after I graduated high school, and he was still there by the time I left for Coast Guard basic training.

It was in this change that Daniel's schooling took a hit. Despite our efforts to keep him mainstreamed, the curriculum differences between his current school and the new one were substantial enough that he would end up being behind for the duration of his schooling. Nevertheless, this was a necessary impact to get the support he truly needed. And most importantly, for him to understand the consequences of his behavior.

...from Daniel's sister (continued)...

We were all kind of ashamed to admit it, but all the times that Daniel was out of the house were like a breath of fresh air. We were finally experiencing what must have been "normal family" status. Our arguments consisted of who was doing the dishes, or where we were going for lunch after church. The tension I was feeling whenever I came home, either from school or work, was suddenly no longer a necessity. The four of us bonded in ways that, unfortunately, simply could not happen while Daniel was in the picture.

We went to visit him a few times while he was in the live-in home, and those were okay if we limited the amount of time we spent there. And the longer he was there, the more my anger and hate towards him drained away, drop by drop.

Seeing him upset and crying whenever it was time for us to go was not easy, and I know now that God was probably grabbing my chin and pointing me towards it, telling me

---

> "Look at him; see his suffering, and know that he needs you." Of course, stubborn old me would still struggle with letting go.

Show them love. The way they receive it.

Suicide and other self-mutilation scenarios are no-joke situations. Those involved need professional help and they need it now. Do not try to work this out on your own. Get them help. Be sensitive and understanding even if you truly do not understand how that could even be in their mind. Get them the help they need. Love them. Value them.

Show them and tell them how much they mean to you. It is a selfish struggle they are going through which can be addressed – but they need help – and they need your support. And they need to be shown love … in the way **they** receive love. Consider a book by Gary Chapman called "The Five Love Languages of Children."[5] This brilliant book, adapted from "The Five Love Languages"[6] (which is in and of itself transformational for marriages), is focused on learning and adapting your methods of engagement with your children so that you stop communicating love in the way **you** understand it (which is our natural approach) and start communicating love in the way **they** understand it.

One additional consideration: I still believe to this day that avoiding things kids will inherently come across in life hinders their maturing process. For example. safety-proofing the home has never been something to which we ascribed. Granted, we made sure poisons were not accessible. But we have always believed that there is a natural consequence to your actions; and educating my kids on that concept will prepare them for a life in this world — not "safety proofing" them from those actions so they never experience the consequences. But we realized that like the poisons and given Daniel's age and resourcefulness, we needed to lock away all the sharp objects as this was well beyond a minor safety concern.

Laughter (funny not funny).

This year we began replacing our kitchen. In the demolition process, I was tearing out the ceiling when a candy wrapper fell on my head. After thinking through what the source might be, I asked Gramma to grab the camera and video the find. As I continued to tear out the ceiling, a plethora of candy wrappers showered over me.

The previous October we had an entire bucket of Halloween candy disappear. As food was a compulsion of Daniel's, and something we continually had to address, this was of little surprise. But it was interesting that this one completely disappeared. Usually, we were pretty good at finding these things. But as time went on, we forgot about it.

...from Daniel...

After taking a full Halloween bucket, I hid all of the candy in my dresser underneath my clean clothes where my mom would never find it.

I was searching for a place to put the wrappers so my parents would not find them either. I was afraid that if they found the wrappers, I would lose privileges and be disciplined. I found the intake vent for the air conditioning system and move the dresser so I could get access to it. I unscrewed the vent (I had taken dad's screwdriver and kept it handy for just such a time) and removed the screws and the vent. And then I promptly used it to "store" all of the wrappers. Eventually, there was so many that I filled up the space. I needed to create more space so I compressed it by shoving my hand down the wall so that I could put more into it (I really never thought about emptying it).

Eventually (about a month later) I ran out of candy and completely forgot about the wrappers ... until dad discovered them when he was working on the kitchen ceiling.

After the incident, I began to connect the dots. The area I was removing was right below Daniel's room – and more specifically, right below the A/C return vent. Because we had not finished all the painting in his room, the vent cover was still removed, and he had apparently opted to use it to hide the wrappers from the candy he had stashed.

As I pulled down the drywall directly below the vent, literally hundreds, if not thousands, of candy wrappers fell out of the ceiling, over my head, and onto the floor. So many, in fact, all of us looking on were in awe. This had clearly been happening for some time for such a collection to take place.

At this point, we could only laugh. Of course, we brought him in and went through the process of understanding why, etc. But the reality is we were laughing so hard because of the sheer volume of candy that he had consumed.

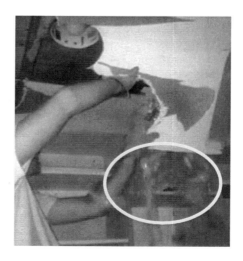

de·ceit /dəˈsēt/ n.

the action or practice of deceiving someone by concealing or misrepresenting the truth.

Deceit is different than lying. Deceit is hidden and can be a common way children hide their wrongdoings. Lying is inappropriate in a different way, but deceit is almost sinister.

We had ultimately landed on the "big 3" or the "3 D's" as a way to express the major character flaws Daniel exposed: Deceit, Defiance, and Disobedience. We had our hands full dealing with these. And because he could not connect action with consequence, these issues were repeated continuously over the years.

"But geez, it's just candy!" Yes, but no. If a kid steals a candy bar at a store, is it "just candy?" No.

Consistently apply your rules. Funny or not, he needed to know his actions were wrong and the deceit of hiding the candy and the wrappers was inappropriate and wrong.

---

[5] Gary Chapman, *The Five Love Languages of Children* (Northfield Publishing, April 15, 2016)

[6] Gary Chapman, *The Five Love Languages*, Reprint edition (Northfield Publishing, January 1, 2015)

Age 16: Scarred, Clotheslined

Rage.

One day I was in Daniel's room addressing what was a pig stye. After finding half gallons of ice cream (melted of course) and a myriad of other foods in his room, along with a conglomeration of verbal disrespect, I blew.

Unfortunately, with me, "blew" meant uncontrolled anger. And that day it surfaced in an ugly and unforgettable way. Daniel had a little bench with a hinged top that could be used for storage. The circumstances culminated with an anger outburst that sent me flipping this piece of furniture over onto his bed. Well, that happened to be right where Daniel was laying, and the corner caught the skin right below his eye.

There is really nothing like the feeling of hurting someone else, especially unintentionally, but most especially when I absolutely know it could have been avoided with more anger control in my life. I felt horrible, and feel horrible to this day, for this event. The shame was deep.

Daniel reacted in pain, of course, but appropriately managed his own anger, and did not react toward me. So, we hopped in the car and went to the emergency room. A couple stitches later and all was well, but now Daniel has a scar visible every time he looks himself in the mirror reminding him of his dad's anger — and more importantly, every time I look at him it reminds me of my failure. Sad really. And so unnecessary.

Scars

Scars are a reminder of actions in our past. Sometimes they represent fun that went awry. Sometimes they bring back the pain of the incident.

Daniel's scar is a constant reminder of the catastrophe that was my anger. And every time I see him, I am visually reminded of that fact. There is no getting around it — I was wrong.

One day we were walking into McDonalds when the frustrations of the day this time took him over-the-top. Now mind you, I was not one to hold back judgment on my children. Many times, I would exasperate them (despite the Biblical mandate not to do so). And when Daniel's anger was rising, I would typically continue to push him to the breaking point – as that strategy typically brought him to a place where he would be willing to listen and work things out. But not today.

Stunned.

Daniel and I got in a disagreement in the car on the way to dinner. When we arrived, we continued the conflict verbally as usual, where we both "stood our ground." I was walking behind him and continuing to push his emotions beyond the brink (rather than trying to diffuse the situation) when his six-foot and 150-pound frame spun around, his arm fully extended, properly clotheslining me across the front of my neck.

I felt the sting of that hit for days to come – and really, I still feel it today. The reality was that this was many years of built-up anger within him that he released in one fell swoop, and literally dropped me to my knees. I suspect his Judo training did not help me much here. While that is not a move he would have learned, the use of force in a smart and effective way is everything that is taught.

Needless to say, he was back in Mt Gretna for about two weeks addressing safety and behavioral issues yet again.

Learning from mistakes

Neither of us have ever hit each other at any other time. I suspect we have both learned our lessons in our own ways recognizing that it should have never happened in either case.

As my children were being raised, I am positive the authorities could have been called on any of us for various reasons. The absence of the call does not make our behaviors right, but an opportunity for a difficult personal lesson. But did you learn it? Or do you keep repeating it?

It is so important to correct our own behavior deficiencies, or there may come a time that someone corrects them for us. We should be growing and striving to get better daily. It is likely that only we know truly what we have done. Work with your spouse and, if necessary, get professional help. The cost will be worth it in the end. Because the cost of not getting help will be substantially more.

Age 17: The Breakthrough

As I look back today, I believe a combination of a new family therapy team and a new age of maturity in Daniel led to a long-needed breakthrough. Our family dynamics were also changing as our daughter was no longer involved in these sessions having moved out to serve our country in the US Coast Guard.

Each team of family therapists kept the normal way of working in process: meeting with Daniel one-on-one at least once-per-week; meeting with the family unit wholly also once-per-week; and meeting with us as parents once-per-week as well. We would go through this cycle for about eight months and then the support would end. He would do okay for a while but without the consistent check-in (a third-party accountability point) he would fall back into his ways and a whole new round would be triggered by a new event that would send him to Mt. Gretna.

The third (and last) team came in after the clothes-lining incident.

...from Daniel's therapist...

My work with Daniel was difficult. I always felt like a periphery character in his life. A side note or added piece of furniture that was novel but easily forgotten. He never became upset or angry at me but when he did in session I always braced inside for the worst and could feel the family's anger and frustration when he would raise his voice and stand up to leave the session.

Daniel and Brad are tall, and their six-foot bodies were intimidating when they stood up. And when Daniel became upset you could feel the room tense and the world slowdown in anticipation for the next "bad thing." I am not sure what helped Daniel start to tolerate family sessions but by the end of our second round he was not leaving the session or refusing to participate. He did not participate when he was in session much, but he was able to be in the room and sustain discussions without verbal aggression.

I believe that it was the work that the family did in reducing their own conflictual approach to Daniel, and Brad and his wife's work in co-parenting and their own emotional regulation. I also think that the tenacity and the Eck's "not-going-to-stop-working-on-this" attitude that slowly eroded the Daniel's fight and helped him see that their approach was an attempt to show love and care for him.

It honestly did not feel any different. We were glad to get the support (clearly better than nothing) but were not at all confident the results would be anything beyond what we had seen previously.

...from Daniel's therapist (continued)...

The rest of the family was still entrenched in their core negative cycle of Daniel "acting out", Brad becoming upset and attempting to set limits and consequences, and the rest of the family attempting to avoid the situation, support Brad, or try to intervene with Daniel.

When I started to work with the family, the Eck's had already been working with another family-based team and I was coming in to fill in for another clinician. I could feel their frustration and sense of defeat at each session and the conflict and exhaustion had taken a toll on Brad and his wife's relationship. The love for each other was not lost but years of fighting and unsuccessful attempts to intervene with Daniel had slowly eroded their desire to communicate, and each attempt at addressing Daniel's behaviors became an invitation for conflict between his parents in their parenting style and approach.

There was a lot of work to be done in helping each family member understand and recognize their role in the negative conflict cycle and to help them establish shared goals and perspective on structure and consequences in the home. With every change in our action, approach, and reaction there is a change in how others react and respond to us.

But something was definitely different. I lean in on his maturity level as having the most impact. Perhaps he physiologically matured past the major aspects of his needs, and perhaps it was something else, but we stopped seeing the compulsion, the disconnect of consequence, and many other aspects of his needs seen over the years.

...from Daniel's therapist (continued)...

The other part of the work that is challenging is the emotional connection and healing that needs to occur in the family, and this was difficult to establish and work on due to the "baggage" and hurt of the past. Daniel struggled to want to engage with his family because in his mind there could be no good outcome of talking about what he did. He expected a lecture, scolding, or exhausted response from his family. His parents struggled to know how to help Daniel understand the emotional impact that his behaviors and actions had and attempts at connection felt forced and fake. However, at some point the family was able to start to engage again, both about Daniel's behaviors and about the impact of each other's reactions.

In the end, I would summarize this year as his development past his special needs. We now deal with a teenage boy on every level.

I suspect he will have remnants of all his issues throughout life, but the breakthrough was less about those issues disappearing and more about his ability to manage them.

...from Daniel's therapist (continued)...

Maturity definitely had something to do with the changes that Daniel was able to make, but without the changes that the family made and without Daniel wanting to work on interacting with his family differently I do not think he would have made the changes that he did on his own accord. I think, also, that the family's values of not giving up and never allowing the feeling of impossibility stop them helped the family persevere through Daniel's challenges and behaviors and helped him see his family as caring rather than punitive and angry.

Time

It can never come fast enough, but the thing about time is it allows for growth. While it is vital to push your children to grow, there is a balance to be found. Give your child the time he needs to grow up.

Daniel may have turned 18, but we found him to be a couple of years behind a typical maturity level emotionally while still fairly on track cognitively.

His breakthrough was after overcoming many phases of difficulty – like storms which need to be weathered individually to come out stronger on the other side. There are times support is appropriate but consider the lesson and do not support in ways that remove the learnings. Children are resilient and capable well beyond what you or they think. Help them work through the problems but let them solve them.

...from Daniel's therapist (continued)...

My individual sessions were often focused on reframing his family and helping Daniel see how much his dad and family loved him. He would often shrug or dismiss my talks about how his family cared about him and how his actions were pushing them away. I do not think that most sessions were helpful to him other than to have someone listen to him, but I remember one session that helped me approach him through a lens that he understood.

There was a riding lawn mower that Daniel was always working on and I was always impressed with Brad when he stated that he did not mind Daniel working on the lawn mower. In my mind I thought of the expense and the possible damage that Daniel could do to the mower, but for

Brad, this was the lesser of the possible things that Daniel could break, and it kept him occupied with something that was controlled and manageable.

While working on the mower, I used the metaphor I often use with families. That family is very much like a machine. Each member, like a part, has a role and depending on their role and function can work harmoniously with the other parts or can break them. I used this when working with Daniel in the hopes of helping him see his role in the core negative sequence and see how his reaction and anger, though helpful to him, was hurting his family and in turn hurting him. I never got a clear response or feeling that he understood or cared about what I said but I hope that something helped him slow down his own reactivity and see his role in the family.

Therapy helps

In all of this, I cannot overstate the benefit of the full family therapeutic approach that Philhaven took. By addressing his needs, the parent's needs, and the family needs all in individual sessions, we were able to zoom in on major areas very specific to those involved and address them directly.

So, get help. But additionally, be teachable. Learn. Adapt. Be better every day. You deserve better. And your child deserves better.

Midway through this year Daniel was accepted into a half-day vocational program at the Lancaster Career and Technology Center – a school dedicated to the growing need of vocational skillsets in our youth. It was fantastic to have Daniel accepted into the program and was a great distraction from the normal classroom. And as it turned out, it was an environment he would thrive in. He started with welding and really fell in love with working with his hands. Rarely did he come home talking about the first part of his day in the classroom, but his whole expression would shine as he expressed the accomplishments he made in welding. It really was fantastic to have him begin to blossom.

Skills

There are a million reasons to consider that skilled labor can be a path for your child. In a world where a premium is put on academia and professionalism, skilled labor is getting lost.

Again, follow your children. Guide their direction while letting them thrive where THEY are capable and passionate. Choosing to pursue a vocational skill or apprenticeship is every bit as important as choosing to be a business professional.

And love them for their choice.

At sixteen, Daniel was not ready emotionally to handle the stresses of driving. And to be honest he was not really interested anyway – so we did not push it. In his time, he would come to us. By the middle of his seventeenth year, he became interested, and the team from Philhaven agreed with us to give it a shot.

Like most things physical, he just connected with driving. He was good at it and he breezed through the training and time required to get his permit. But as we know, it is rarely how good we are at something that bites us – it is the weak points.

For Daniel, his weaknesses were found in distractions and a struggle to focus. One day as we were heading off fishing, he was looking for the road in which to turn. He slowed down but continued to struggle to find it until it was almost too late and, due to the speed of the car coming at him over a blind hill, made the turn without seeing the risk. This, his first accident, was a head-on collision totaling both cars.

He and I were fine as our car did an amazing job absorbing the impact. However, the other couple were both taken away in an ambulance. It was truly not intentional, and the blind hill and their speed did not help the situation. Nevertheless, Daniel struggled with this one emotionally for a while. And physically every month when he must pay his ever-increasing insurance bill.

Daniel loves to drive and does so everywhere despite it killing his pocketbook. It seems at times this is the only reason he works ... so he can drive.

Accidents

Our kids make mistakes. Let them. In time they learn that wisdom (learning from others' mistakes) is better than experience (learning from your own) and will adjust accordingly.

But accidents are just that. No ill intent. If your kid spills their milk at the dinner table, they do not deserve a lashing, but a calm corrective engagement. If they total your car, who cares, it is just a car. Your kid's life means so much more. And how you handle these situations will leave a forever imprint on their lives.

Age 18: Just Another Teenage Boy

> **Proverbs 22:6 (MSG):**
>
> *"Point your kids in the right direction—when they're old they won't be lost."*

Senior year! Did we really make it here? We began to see the light at the end of the tunnel in relation to struggling through his growing up years. For the first time, we saw that he might get to the point of being able to make it on his own. And for the first time, his mom and I began to think that we might experience an empty nest. In many ways the thought was exciting, and in many nerve-wrecking, but in the end our goal was to get him to the point where this was possible, and for the first time we could see success around the corner.

The first girlfriend came along and really showed us that he was well-shy of a maturity level that could manage such emotional impact – good or bad. Of course, it did not help that his first choice was also one struggling through special needs issues of her own.

Perhaps they could help each other?

But the reality is that is not why a relationship should exist.

Through this whole time, we encouraged Daniel to keep asking why: "Why are you in a relationship?"; "Why this one?"; "What's the end-game?"; etc. We all know that logic loses when love is in play, and this relationship was no exception. It lasted for quite some time, but in the end their selfishness clashed and destroyed the relationship.

And that will continue until each of them realize that relationships only thrive when selfishness dies.

Selfishness

Relationships are hard.

And we are naturally selfish.

A successful love relationship thrives in the concept of "dying to self" - e.g., putting your partner's needs before your own.

And you must do it daily. Nay, hourly. Nay, always. When you get in the way, you degrade your partner.

None of us are great at this. It is a life pursuit. But it is one that will be rewarded. Rewarded daily. Nay, hourly. Nay, always.

Consider, however, that having parents that are trained in specific areas children are struggling to learn cannot be easy for a kid. Teenagers inherently do not want to listen to us, but will seek out advice elsewhere, almost even intending to find a counter-opinion.

In our case, it was relationships. And Daniel was no exception. He did not want to listen or think through these questions when hormones are raging, and selfishness is peaking.

Be sure, though, your kids hear you. But they will likely not acknowledge it, nor show it landed. Be ahead of this - talk with them early and often (especially when they are not emotionally engaged in the issue) and are willing to listen.

Excited.

This was the year Daniel was accepted into CTC's full-time automotive mechanic program. And he absorbed it. It was quite a stunning revelation to have him work through this one. He was never a reader – but he read automotive books.

In one year of school that was intended really to only teach him the surface capabilities, he dug deep on his own.

He bought his first car, a really cool Explorer that had a Jurassic Park wrap on it, and he dug into it to rebuild the engine.

In time, he would get a good summer job, buy another Explorer to use as parts, and continue to work to get the truck functional. Automotive repair, alongside fishing, became his passion and he was consistently found doing one or the other.

Find their passion

Help your kids find their passion and empower them to pursue it. How many times have we heard from kids that their parent wanted them to be a doctor, or a football player, or a <whatever>? Who gives a rip what you think – it is not your life;

it is your child's. And God made them to fulfill a unique role in this world — one that He did not tell you, and one that He will reveal to His child directly. So, work through it with your kids. Help them find what they are good at and then do everything in your power to open the doors, so they have the opportunity to excel in that area.

*By the way, it helps if you know yours. Why are you here? What is your purpose on this planet? Pursue it and find it. It is so much easier to teach someone how to do something when you know how yourself. Better yet, work through this **with** your kids so they experience the process.*

In lieu of the *gift* a parent might provide to their child in the form of a car or college (major costs here in America), my wife and I agreed early on that we would do something a bit different to celebrate their graduation. In that, we would offer to take that child to a destination of their choosing anywhere in the world. This gift would be something they would not likely be able to do on their own in a very long time and would provide them with values and memories that they could not otherwise obtain.

174 | Brad Eck

> *...from Daniel...*
>
> *While I was at Hoffman, they had a small pond across the street. I asked my dad to bring me his fishing pole and some equipment so he could take advantage of fishing over there. It was then I fell in love with fishing. I had always enjoyed fishing, but it was at Hoffman where it became something I would really pursue.*
>
> *Upon returning home, I would save my money from side jobs and eventually bought a fishing kayak. I started making flies, collecting different lures, and every dime I spent would in some way tie back to fishing.*

Daniel's passion for fishing took him to Alaska for his graduation trip. So, at 18, he packed his bags and the three of us trekked up toward the Great Frontier. As Mama loves cruising, we booked a cruise one-way from Vancouver through the inner passageway and ended in Seward.

Excitement.

We fished land and sea for a few days, experienced driving ATVs in the back woods, and just generally played. We caught a lot of halibut out on the charter one day and packed it up for shipping home.

He really had a time packed full of memories and it helped to fuel his passion even further. The trip was amazing, and we had a good relational experience with each other – minimal anger and frustration and just the enjoyment of spending time together. These were types of experiences we did not often have. He and I both have begun to recognize our triggers and initiate our own "safety plans" to manage or exit the situation.

Airplanes not helicopters

As parents, we need to act like airplanes and not like helicopters with our children – "jetting" them to their next destination, not hovering over them.

Our children were raised knowing they would be responsible for all costs when buying anything they wanted (not needed). This was a learned value for us, and we determined as parents early on that forwarding that legacy was the right way to best prepare them for the world. And it supported the idea that we implanted in them from day one: our kids are responsible for who they are and who they become. This mindset of preparation for the real world covers every area of life, including finances.

And we really did not have exceptions to this.

Many parents feel responsible to provide for their kids' post-high school education (in America this is a personal cost of great *expense). Many others feel it is giving their kids a head-start that they perhaps were not afforded. But ours knew early on that if they wanted college, they would have to find their own way to pay for it. To us, this decision was never really about the cost, but about the responsibility we were developing in them.*

Additionally, we would also never buy a vehicle for them, or pay their insurances, or buy a phone, etc. These are costs that teach them responsibility. They even had to pay rent to us after graduation if they stayed in our home.

Now within those rules there is plenty of flexibility in how they might make it happen. All three of our kids pulled a loan from us for their first car. But this also allowed us to teach them how the whole financial process works real world. We required a down payment, we established an interest rate, and we agreed on default terms. Our youngest figured this out, did it early on (at sixteen) and we even ended up leasing the car back from him because he could not even drive yet!

Instead of going directly to college after high school, our daughter opted to go into the United States Coast Guard. This allowed her to qualify for the education benefits paid for by the government. Both of our sons opted for vocational skills training instead of formal college.

In the end, the goal is to get your children to a place of self-sufficiency: not relying on us, the government, or anyone else. Learning this early gives them the gift of self-reliance: something that cannot be taught by parents paying their way for anything.

Age 19 (and Beyond): Life

Daniel was not much interested in going to school. But he had a serious interest in the Army over the course of his young life. To his frustration, however, he found out that he could not get in the Army if he were on any medications. In fact, he had to be off them for a full year before they would consider him.

So, he did!

Not in the best way, but one day we were checking on him and he told us he had stopped his meds about a month prior. Frustrated (as he should have weaned off them slowly) but accepting his desires, we watched him closely for a while to make sure he could manage. He still has his mood swings, but in time he will work through these and self-manage. In a way, we are proud he had the gall to make this happen. We would have known early on if things got out of hand, but he handled the transition well.

Now, the Army being who they are, then promptly told him he could not qualify if there was any mental health history. That sent us reeling with disappointment. His interest in any of the branches and military quickly expired after that point.

It is unfortunate; he is a strong kid with a lot of potential and eliminating someone from anything based on their past and not their present is truly a sad way to do business.

Leveraging disappointment

Disappointments in life are bound to happen. As your children grow, do not skim by these lightly. Take advantage of them as teaching opportunities. Teach them to accept defeat, but to grit through it, learn a lesson, and pursue a new path.

And by all means, do not let them give up when they experience failure or disappointment. If they choose to go a different direction later, so be it, but do not let them stop amid defeat.

Perseverance, courage, determination, diligence, steadfastness, etc. are all excellent characteristics your children can learn if they learn to fight though disappointment. Be their example! Talk to them about your own life and the struggles you face. They learn more from you by watching than they do from listening.

Where Daniel goes from here is an unknown. But what we do know is that he is as ready as ever. We never thought we would be able to say anything near that, but he has grown up. He is putting aside his manipulative ways and becoming a man in which his parents can be truly proud. He is grounded in his beliefs and understands the importance of doing right in this world. Be blessed my son. You are loved.

Letting go

You are never ready to really let go of your children. Ironically enough, you never are really ready to have them in the first place. We grow and we adapt and that is really the key message Daniel has taught us over the years. We invest our time, our resources, and frankly, our lives into the kids. And then we pray and hope they take that base and live a fruitful and good life.

For us, we committed them early on into the hands of God for His use. And we pray often that their will ultimately aligns with His plan for them. For it is then where they will truly be effective and beneficial in this world.

Afterword

...from Daniel's mom...

I am well aware that many of you readers are wondering why I did not include anything in my husband's story about Daniel. To put it simply, I am just not ready yet to bear my heart on the subject of Daniel. Raising him has been the most difficult and emotional responsibility I have ever experienced. I am ashamed and embarrassed of the different ways I tried to cope over the years. My responsibility in teaching him how to be as functional and healthy as possible will not end until the day I die.

Unfortunately, there are many days when I feel like I have failed miserably. My logical brain simply does not understand how Daniel can continue to repeat terrible decisions. It has become easier for me to not be involved in his adult life, which should not be the case.

My faith in Jesus, some mental therapy, and my dear soul sisters are the things that keep me going. Perhaps one day I can open up to readers and dive into the hard times from a mom's perspective.

Daniel's special needs issues were unexpected. 25 years ago, if you would have asked me, there is no way I would have anticipated going through the wealth of experiences created by having a special needs kid.

But I also would not change it for anything.

It has been tough. Nay, beyond tough. There are times when I look back wondering how we ever made it through.

And, oh the times of personal failure.

This is not a journey I would wish on anyone. But God is sovereign. He knows for what we are capable. And He knows that if we lean into Him, nothing is impossible.

...from Daniel's sister...

Growing up as the oldest of three children can be hard enough. Growing up with a younger brother with mental disabilities can be incredibly difficult. Growing up with a brother with mental disabilities and extreme anger, violence, and selfishness can be devastating. I know that God was able to keep us together as a family because nothing else would have been able to do so.

Through this book we used stories of raising Daniel, and our own personal experiences through those incidents, to express lessons of parenting and life. From dealing with personal issues of anger and marriage incompatibilities, to the dangers of isolation and disobedience, we have journeyed through these ordeals together and explored not only the emotional impact of the events, but the underlying principles that allow us to apply practical application to situations we face in life.

...from Daniel's sister (continued)...

Unfortunately, our family will never be what we could be. We all still struggle daily with the effects of being a family with a special needs kid. My mother, youngest brother, and I have all reacted in a very similar way: we have shutdown.

Our emotions were so completely destroyed during Daniel's growth that we found our own survival in shutting ourselves away. For my parents, this has caused major struggles within their marriage as well as their relationship with us as their kids. For my youngest brother, this has caused him to not only shut away his emotions, but to shut himself away from everyone altogether.

I cannot understate the importance of many of these lessons. Some of you will find these equally as impactful and some you may choose to disagree and ignore – after all, these are *our* experiences, not yours. I just encourage you to consider the perspective, recognizing none of us are trained, professional parents but are consistently learning along the way, reading, and studying how to be better every day.

> *...from Daniel's sister (continued)...*
>
> For me, I struggle in my own marriage to find the middle ground between total shutdown and total lash out. Daniel's actions, and my own in response, have had consequences extending well beyond me leaving the home. I struggle relationally in every way possible, with every relationship possible. I have never been able to maintain friendships, my relationships with my family are tense at best, and my marriage is under fire every day.

But through all this there is one element where I take an unapologetic stand; and that is the impact of God in our lives. Long before we had children, my wife and I had developed a personal relationship with Christ and had seen Him move in amazing ways in our lives both individually, as a couple, and ultimately as a family.

...from Daniel's sister (continued)...

I am not going to sit here and tell you that it is easy to work through something like this. I am not going to tell you that you will not be a changed person. I am not going to tell you that it will all be better eventually. But I can tell you that the strength, compassion, and peace you need can *only* be found in God. I struggle in my relationship with God every. Single. Day. I struggle to trust Him. I struggle to feel loved by Him. But I also know that He is with me. Every. Single. Day.

My relationship with Daniel will always be rocky. We will have our times of anger and fighting, and quite possibly violence. But at the end of the day, he is my brother. And while I will always struggle to portray my love for him in the right way, I know that my prayers to God will not go unanswered, and I know that He can bridge the gap between my brother and me.

Our experience has underscored the daily influence God has in our lives and solidified our dependence on Him. We are fully convinced the journey to raise Daniel would have gone substantially different without God's guidance.

Yes, I waivered. Yes, I sinned. Yes, I am a failure. But with Christ's forgiveness and second chances (i.e., grace), I got back up and tried again. And again. And again.

As we pursued this journey together, my wife and I struggled in more ways than imaginable. And our unwavering commitment to God and each other kept us moving forward ... together.

He is sufficient for *all* our needs. He can bear the weight of our burdens. He is the foundation of everything in our lives.

And He can be yours too.

Just ask Him.

About the Author

Brad Eck has a background in software engineering, management, and partner engagement in various industries. Expanding his career toward people leadership in 2017, he completed an Executive MBA program. He and his wife made reality their long-time dream of purchasing a bed and breakfast in 2019 in Southeast Pennsylvania. Having been trained in marriage mentorship, leadership of men, and student and children ministries, his passion for investing in others continues to underpin everything he does. He still works full time as an eco-system manager all the while pursuing his passion of investing in others by mentoring, writing, and engaging with others through the venue of their B&B. You can find him at @authorbradeck on Facebook, Twitter, and LinkedIn.

About the Contributors

Story contributions:

    Abby Printz: Daniel's older sister

    Benji Eck: Daniel's younger brother

    Daniel Eck

    Cindy Eck: Daniel's mother

    Shirley Kohl: Daniel's paternal grandmother

    Eddie Eck: Daniel's paternal grandfather

    Jeff Johnson, LMFT: therapist and family friend

Illustrations:

    David Lock

Cover Design:

    Danielle Smith-Boldt

Editors:

    Amber Hatch

    Abby Printz

Thank you to all who contributed and supported me in the effort to write this book. Thanks to the many (who may have identified themselves in these stories) whose positive influence helped us persevere. And thanks most to God who gave us the strength to persevere in this journey.